PASSOVER EDITION

BROOKE ARMY MEDICAL CENTER
FORT SAM HOUSTON, TEXAS
BROOKE GENERAL HOSPITAL

HAPP

Passover

by
Rabbi David I. Golovensky

*T*HIS is one in a series of Jewish inspirational pamphlets published for personnel of the Jewish faith in the Armed Forces of the United States by the National Jewish Welfare Board — a member agency of the United Service Organizations.

NATIONAL JEWISH WELFARE BOARD
145 East 32nd Street, New York 16, New York

סדר
הגדה של פסח

מה נשתנה הלילה הזה מכל הלילות?

New York,
Druck u. Verlag der H. Frank's Buchdruckerei, 205 Houston St.
1851.

Passover Feast: Blessing over the wine

FOR A FREE PALESTINE
AMERICAN LEAGUE

הגדה של פסח

American
Heritage
Haggadah

American Heritage Haggadah

The Passover Experience

Compiled and Edited by David Geffen
English Translation by Moshe Kohn
Introduction by Stuart E. Eizenstat

gefen
publishing house בית הוצאה לאור

Jerusalem 1992/5752

Photo Typeset by Gefen Ltd.

Cover Design and Graphics: Gila Nidam

ISBN 965-229-083-1

Edition 9 8 7 6 5 4 3 2

Gefen Publishing House Ltd.   Gefen Books
POB 6056, Jerusalem   POB 101, Woodmere
91060 Israel   N.Y., U.S.A. 11598

Photo on back cover: The rabbi oversees the baking of matzah in New York
in 1858. Frank Leslie's Illustrated Newspaper, April 10, 1858.
Ezra P. Gorodesky Collection.

Printed in Jerusalem, Israel

סדר
הגדה של פסח.

SERVICE

FOR THE

TWO FIRST NIGHTS

OF

PASSOVER,

HEBREW AND ENGLISH.

FOURTH EDITION.

NEW-YORK,

HENRY FRANK, PRINTER AND PUBLISHER.

No. 3 Cedar Street.

1857.

In order to maintain the authentic character of the source material, all quotations and citations have been left in their original form.

The Hebrew Text

The Hebrew text of the American Heritage Haggadah was photographed from a Hebrew-English Haggadah printed in New York in 1857.

The copy from which the photograph was made is in the Jewish National and University Library in Jerusalem.

That text was used because it was one of the earliest Haggadot published in the United States.

No changes were made throughout the Haggadah, though a few variations were identified. The text was maintained to preserve its authenticity.

The variations are of two types. The first is different usage of the Hebrew voweling. The second is omissions of parts of the text.
We indicate these omissions with an asterisk.
The following are the omissions:

Page 62:   * רַבּוֹתַי נְבָרֵךְ

Page 66:   * הָרַחֲמָן הוּא יְבָרֵךְ אוֹתִי וְאֶת אִשְׁתִּי וְאֶת זַרְעִי וְאֶת כָּל אֲשֶׁר לִי.

Page 66:   * נַעַר הָיִיתִי גַם זָקַנְתִּי וְלֹא רָאִיתִי צַדִּיק נֶעֱזָב וְזַרְעוֹ מְבַקֶּשׁ לָחֶם.

Page 79:   * וְשַׂמְּחֵנוּ בְּיוֹם חַג הַמַּצּוֹת הַזֶּה.

Developing The American Heritage Haggadah

*A*merican liberty has stamped many Jewish hearts with a Kosher for Passover seal, and for many people Passover has an American connotation. As a student of Haggadot with an American flavor, the publication of an American Heritage Haggadah seemed a logical step for me. How did my perspective on the America-Passover relationship develop?

In the late 1940s and during the 1950s, I attended sedarim together with my parents at my grandparents' home in Atlanta, Georgia. My grandfather, Rabbi Tobias Geffen, introduced me to Pesach via his traditional rendering of the Haggadah. Garbed in a white kittel robe and with his flowing beard, my Zaide chanted each and every word using the melodies he had learned as a youth at his home in Kovno, Lithuania.

Though the chanting of the Haggadah at those sedarim still echoes in my ears, it was the culmination of the seder that most deeply impressed me. My Bubbie, Rebbetzin Sara Hene Geffen, orchestrated the final part of the evening. After "Had Gadya," she initiated the singing of "Hatikvah," "The Star Spangled Banner" and "God Bless America." Deeply aware of the Holocaust tragedy that had decimated her Eastern European family, she knew that the U.S.A. had provided her, her husband, their children and grandchildren with the blessings of freedom. Her feelings touched a personal responsive chord, and Pesach, the season of our liberation, became for me an American Jewish celebration. In retrospect, the idea of an American Heritage Haggadah germinated during those sedarim, but the process took over three decades to incubate and evolve into the present volume.

The American Jewish community, the largest single concentration of Jews in one country, has distinguished itself in many areas throughout its three-and-a-half-century existence. This includes contributions to both general and Jewish art and literature.

However, the Haggadah, the Jewish book with the largest number of copies in print in the United States, presents an interesting paradox. While hundreds of editions of the Haggadah have been created in the United States, very few American Haggadot have appeared.

What is an "American Haggadah"? I define it as a Haggadah in which the visual and documentary material and interpretive notes reflect the American approach to Passover.

Through my research in American Jewish history, I discovered graphic and verbal material relevant to the portrayal of the Passover experience in the U.S.A. The first rendition of an "American Haggadah" was the 1879 Liberman-Chicago edition. The author's introduction focused on local holiday customs and the artist's depictions of the search for leaven and the "Four Sons" reflected contemporary American Jewish life in that Midwestern city. In contrast, only European drawings were included in other illustrated nineteenth-century American Haggadot.

The news media present other visual records of Passover in America in the previous century. Most attention was directed to the baking of matzah, the key Passover staple. The earliest illustrations are from 1852 and 1858, the first appearing in an Anglo-Jewish newspaper and the second in a general weekly newspaper.

The celebration of Passover in America in 1889 made the newspapers. In that year, the centennial of George Washington's inauguration as president, a drawing of a family observing the holiday shows how the "Father of His Country" had been integrated into the heart and soul of the seder. His picture was hung prominently in many American Jewish homes, and Washington's letters to American Jews were read at the seder demonstrating how closely knit American and Jewish identities had become.

V

From the earliest years of this century, Passover in America is best understood through the wide variety of advertisements that appeared in Anglo-Jewish and general English newspapers, in the Yiddish and Hebrew press, in cookbooks and in Haggadot. The holiday necessitated a different diet with the exacting preparation of commercial foodstuffs, and the marketing of these products was directed at the American housewife. Food manufacturers offered free Passover cookbooks or sold them inexpensively in order to encourage purchase of their merchandise.

The Haggadah emerged as a major marketing device from the first decade of the twentieth century. They were sponsored by banks, butcher shops, caterers, soft drink concerns, coffee and wine companies, travel agencies and other providers of consumer goods and services.

In the 1930s, another form of advertising emerged. Hotels in New York, New Jersey and Michigan publicized their Passover accommodations. After World War II, the hotels in Florida and the Catskill Mountains began to attract clientele, eventually becoming major locales for celebrating the Passover away from home.

Jews have always served in the U.S. military, and it was essential that they be provided with proper foods for the seder. Records of military sedarim exist as early as the Civil War and for all the wars of this century. Jews serving in the continental USA or other parts of the world were supplied with their Passover needs even if it meant bringing the food in by dogsled in Alaska. During the 1991 Persian Gulf War, eight Jewish chaplains, from all branches of the service, conducted sedarim in Kuwait, Saudi Arabia, on warships in the Persian Gulf and on the Cunard Princess docked in Bahrain.

Clearly, in any undertaking of this type, selection must be judicious and not all available material could be included. Only a few Passover art objects are presented, but one is very special, an Ilya Schor Passover plate in silver commissioned by a family in Baltimore, Maryland in 1956. The fields of music and cinema are under-represented, though the patriotism of Passover is evident in a Yiddish song from the first decade of the twentieth century. Nor can one forget the 1914 silent movie, "Passover Miracle." In a powerful scene, the son, who had married out of the faith, finally returns home, arriving as the door is opened for Elijah.

The American Heritage Haggadah, with a new English translation and a photographed 1857 New York Hebrew text, attempts to weave together lesser known but striking dimensions of the American Passover experience. Explore the American Passover ambience by viewing matzah machines of the 1850s, an 1859 seder and the "Train Seder" of 1919, and by reading about Passover in San Francisco in 1851, the Georgia Chain Gang "matzah pardon" of 1933 and the Congressional hearing on the "mailing of matzoh" in 1972.

This volume draws upon the wellsprings of faith, commitment and love exemplified in the lives of my parents, Anna and Louis Geffen, and my in-laws, Frieda and David Feld. May God bless each of them with many more special years.

A Haggadah of this nature can come into being only when one has the opportunity to conduct his own family sedarim. Our children, Avie, Jeremy and Elissa, our son-in-law, Chemi, and our grandson, Ori, have brought much joy to my wife, Rita, and me around the seder table both in the U.S.A. and, after aliyah, in Jerusalem. Their questions make me consider anew the meaning of Passover.

This Haggadah is lovingly dedicated to my wife, Rita. She encouraged and supported me from the project's inception to its completion, and her multi-faceted suggestions have proved invaluable. She has been a continuous source of inspiration, and this volume is hers as much as it is mine.

David Geffen
Jerusalem
Hanukka 5752
December 1991

Rabbi Dr. David Geffen made aliyah with his family in 1977 and is a resident of Jerusalem. He received a BA from Emory University, a PHD from Columbia University and was ordained at the Jewish Theological Seminary of America.

VI

The Seder and the Haggadah

*E*very Seder has a special meaning, and every Seder in my parents' home as I was growing up in my native New York had an extra-special meaning for me and my seven siblings. When we concluded the Seder with the singing of "Next year in Jerusalem," we meant it in a very direct, personal way: my parents, Rabbi Zvi Hersch and Leah (Sternberger) Kohn, had only recently arrived in New York from Jerusalem, together with my older sister. They were part of the great migration of tens of thousands of Jews and Arabs — some 10 percent of the population of what was then called Palestine — who left during and in the wake of World War I, when the country was in turmoil and there wasn't enough food and work to go around. They went to the U.S.A, and other countries, where they hoped to find a livelihood for themselves plus something to send back to their parents and siblings in Palestine, and something to set aside for their early return home.

It took my parents 42 years to return home to Jerusalem to live out their days. Meanwhile, our home in New York was in reality a faraway annex, so to speak, of Jerusalem. For we were the only branch of my parents' large families living in the U.S.A., and all that we children knew about grandparents, uncles, aunts and cousins was very directly associated with Jerusalem, an association that in those years was maintained only through letters. So when, at the conclusion of the Seder, we sang "Next year in Jerusalem," it had a direct, personal meaning for us. Quite a few Sedarim came and went, including one in 1945 at the Allied military base at Myitkyina in the North Burma jungle where I was serving in the U.S. Signal Corps, before I finally celebrated my first Passover at home. It was only at Passover 1958 that for the first time we sang the "home version" of that closing song, "Next year in Jerusalem-Rebuilt."

At that Passover Seder — shortly after I, my wife and our three U.S.-born children had "gone up" from Chicago and New York to Jerusalem (where our fourth child was born a year later) — we did not have to stretch our imagination to perform the key act of the Seder. That act is the sociodrama our lawgivers command us to perform: "In every generation every person is to regard himself as having personally gone out of Egypt" — out of any state of bondage or lack of sovereignty.

The scenario, as it were, for that sociodrama is the Haggadah, which is Hebrew for "telling."

Probably no book in the world besides the Bible has so engaged the mind and imagination of scholars, popular commentators, illustrators, printers and collectors as the Haggadah. More than 3,500 different editions have been catalogued, new editions keep being published, numerous reprints of these editions keep appearing, and from time to time an old Haggadah whose existence was unknown comes to light.

As indicated, the Haggadah gives the basic order to be followed at the Seder (Hebrew for "order" or "arrangement") and the cues for our enactment of what I have called the Passover sociodrama. It is all based on the same passage in the Torah. Here is how the Haggadah sums up what the Sages instruct us in tractate Pessahim 116b:

> In every generation every person is to regard himself as having personally been redeemed from Egyptian bondage, for it is written (Exodus 13:8): "And you shall tell your child on that day, saying: 'This is because of what God did for me when I went free from Egypt.' " So we see that God redeemed

not only "them," our ancestors, but also us, as written (Deuteronomy 6:23): "And He [God] brought us out of there [Egypt] to bring us into the Land that He promised to our ancestors."

The question arises: What is the "this" referred to in Exodus 13:8? The Haggadah itself gives the answer, earlier in the "telling." Immediately after the description of the four different types of sons, the Haggadah tells us, quoting from the Talmudic Midrash known as the Mechilta (section "Bo" 17):

Since the Torah commands us (Exodus 13:5) to observe the Passover rites "in this month [Nissan]," we might suppose that we ought to do so from the very first day of the month. So the Torah specifies (Exodus 13:8) "on that day," the day on which the Passover is celebrated. But if "day," then why do we do so at night? Because in the last passage, the father is instructed to reply to his child: "This is because..." — "this" referring to the matzah and the bitter herb that are set on the table before you when you do the telling.

So the central purpose of the Seder, which is the high point of the Passover celebration, is the "telling" — the telling of the story of our birth as a nation when we were liberated from slavery in Egypt. And the "telling" opens, immediately after a youngster at the Seder table has asked the Four Question, by quoting Deuteronomy 6:21: "...We were slaves to Pharaoh in Egypt and God, our god, brought us out of there with a mighty hand." That opening passage of the "telling" goes on to impress upon us the importance of telling the story again and again — no matter how learned and clever we are, we should never tire of repeating this story of our emergence from slavery to freedom and nationhood.

Now the telling need not be — ought not be — a rote repetition of what is printed in this or in any other Haggadah. In our day, especially, a Jew doesn't have to "pretend" to have been personally redeemed. There is hardly a Jew alive who has not personally experienced or who does not have a close relative who has experienced some part of our people's classic slavery-redemption story: the Holocaust; persecution in Eastern Europe and many Arab lands; the re-establishment of the Jewish state in the Land of Israel; the liberation of the Jews of Eastern Europe and the Arab lands; the liberation of the Jews of Ethiopia — there is hardly a Jew alive who does not have a personal story to tell about his or her experiences in the numerous Jewish sagas of our days, or who does not have a story to pass on after hearing it from someone close.

Let the Haggadah not be a mere script to be repeated as printed. Let it rather be the outline guiding our telling of our ancestral Passover story and the list of cues signalling us to enrich the time-honored "telling" by adding to it our own, personal Passover stories and thoughts.

With praise and thanks to the Supreme Author; to my parents, of blessed memory, who made me an Eretz Yisrael Jew; to my wife, Dvora-Barbara, whose partnership has been of inestimable value in my remaining one; and to my children and their partners and children, through whom we pray we shall forever continue our Eretz Yisrael partnership.

Moshe Kohn
Jerusalem
Hanukka 5752
December 1991

Moshe Kohn is a veteran "Jerusalem Post" writer and editor and has translated many prose and poetical works from Hebrew and Yiddish into English.

Introduction

*D*r. David Geffen has done the Jewish community of the United States a wonderful service by developing the first modern, authentically American Passover Haggadah, fusing American history with the timeless Jewish story of the Exodus from Egypt in the thirteenth century B.C.E.

The Passover Seder is by far the most observed American Jewish practice. What accounts for the remarkable level of observance of Passover by American Jews? What is there about the Passover story that holds so much interest for the American Jewish community?

The American Heritage Haggadah beautifully suggests the reasons.

First, the Exodus story portrayed in the Haggadah, which is central to Passover, is the seminal event in Jewish history. Thus, Jews in the United States, like those in Israel and throughout the world, would naturally wish to remember and symbolically re-enact this event. The movement of Jews from the slavery of Egypt through the Sinai wandering for forty years to the freedom of the Promised Land is the transforming experience in Jewish history.

It is the Exodus that shaped Judaism as an enduring religion; that created a Jewish community of shared values; that began the process of Jewish nationhood; that demonstrated God's intention for the Jewish people to have a unique mission in history; that led to the giving of the Ten Commandments and the Torah that has shaped the special Jewish sensitivity to the disadvantaged, the poor, the stranger — "because we were strangers in Egypt."

The redemption from Egypt has shaped over 3,000 years the Jewish precept that man's betterment comes not from the after-life but from improvement in the human condition here on earth.

It is not coincidental that polls repeatedly taken of the political attitudes of American Jewry demonstrate an unprecedented identification with progressive views toward low-income Americans, civil rights for minorities and intervention to assist the disadvantaged. The concept of the tithe, the sabbatical year and Jubilee year when land is to be returned to its owner, the cancellation of debts, the antipathy toward slavery all emanate from the Passover and Sinai experience, embodied in the Torah and in prophets such as Isaiah.

Second, the Passover Seder and the reading of the Haggadah is quintessentially a family event and the family has been the foundation of Judaism from time immemorial. We each have our own Seder family memories. Mine begin as a young child when our whole family would assemble around my Aunt Ida's dining-room table, led by my father, Leo, who was deeply steeped in Judaic knowledge. The Seder was conducted almost entirely in Hebrew; the women in the family, including my mother, Sylvia, were not expected to join in the rapid recitation of the Passover story.

But there was one point of the Haggadah at which my father would stop for emphasis and expound on its importance. It was when the Haggadah stresses that we today are to view ourselves as if we were slaves in Egypt, that each generation should feel itself personally redeemed from Egypt. It is this personal feeling of going through the process from slavery to freedom that my father insisted we all understand. It is this which infuses the social consciousness of American Jews today.

When I married my wife, Fran, had children, Jay and Brian, and began to lead Seders, first in Atlanta, later in Washington, I was determined to have a more participatory Seder, but one that retained the richness and Jewish flavor of those my father led. I work hard each year, drawing on interpretations from a variety of sources.

By far the most memorable Seder was one in which the President of the United States and his wife, Jimmy and Rosalynn Carter, joined us. When we came to the portion of the Seder in which I was to pour the cup of wine and welcome the Prophet Elijah, I got up and started to open the front door. A Secret Service agent jumped up and stopped me, saying that for security reasons the door could not be opened. My entreaties failed to move him. As a compromise, I was able to persuade him to permit me to open our rear door — the only time Elijah has been relegated to the back door in my home.

There is another reason why Passover has such a powerful hold on American Jews, one particularly relevant to the American experience. As the American Heritage Haggadah magnificently displays, Passover's central message of freedom for Jews from Egyptian bondage and, implicitly, the possibility of freedom for all mankind resonates with the American experience of fighting a revolution for freedom from England. Indeed, from the earliest days of our own republic and its struggle for freedom, the leadership of our emerging nation cited the Israelite exodus from Egypt as a historical model. In 1776, Benjamin Franklin, Thomas Jefferson and John Adams wanted to portray Moses leading the Children of Israel through the Red Sea as the ideal of freedom that should be displayed on the Great Seal of the United States, with the proposed motto, "Rebellion to Tyrants is Obedience to God." Thomas Jefferson, the third President of the United States, made this his personal seal.

We see in the American Heritage Haggadah how the thread of American history has been woven into Passover's message of freedom. In the early part of this century, Passover was referred to as the Jewish Fourth of July.

Quite interesting are the many ties between American history and Passover, going back to the earliest days of the country. You will find in this Haggadah dramatic illustrations and stories such as that of Gershom Mendes Seixas, the hazzan of New York's Shearith Israel Congregation, who fled to Philadelphia with this family when the British took over New York during the Revolutionary War. In 1784, after the War was concluded, he was expected to return to this position in New York by Passover time. In a letter to the synagogue president he said he would come if necessary, himself, but noted that "it is difficult for a man to be away from his family for Pesach."

The printing of the Haggadah began in the United States in 1837 and has continued unabated since then. Before, Haggadot had come from England. Two 1815 English Haggadot bear the names of members of the Jefferson Levy family. Levy lived at Thomas Jefferson's Monticello after the death of his uncle, Commodore Uriah P. Levy, who had purchased Monticello from Jefferson's heirs. Annually, Seders were held at Monticello and the Haggadot with their Passover wine stains bear witness to the Jewish celebration of freedom in the home of perhaps the greatest American of all time.

We see in the American Heritage Haggadah the earliest depiction of the Seder in America, in a drawing on "The Rites and Worship of the Hebrews" published in 1859 by Max Wolff, recently displayed in the Library of Congress collection of Judaica. We note the father, wearing a high hat, telling the story of the Exodus to this young child sitting in a high chair, demonstrating the transmission of this seminal event in Jewish history from one generation to the next.

In 1889, on the centennial of George Washington's inauguration as America's first President, the George Washington Seder was held. During that centennial year, free pictures of Washington were given for every purchase of ten pounds of matzah. As seen in the illustration in the American Heritage Haggadah, our first President is shown near the door awaiting Elijah's arrival. What a wonderful integration of Americana with Judaica!

In more recent times, the Seder has been widely observed in the United States military during World Wars I and II, the Korean and Vietnam Wars, and, only recently, the Persian Gulf War on Arab territory. The largest Seder in the Persian Gulf military theater was held for 400 Jewish military personnel on a Navy ship off Bahrain. As the American Heritage Haggadah vividly indicates, the Haggadah has been used to express

support for a variety of American political issues, from the advocacy of the rights of blacks and migrants, to women's liberation, to a Vegetarian Haggadah.

One remarkable quality of the American Seder service is its adaptability to new events in Jewish history. The recent Seder rituals created by American Jewry for remembering the six million Jews killed during the Holocaust, and for expressing solidarity with the plight of the Soviet and Ethiopian Jews, have helped bind us to our brothers and sisters around the world and energized us to work for their freedom as Moses worked for the freedom of the Jews in Egypt around 1225 B.C.E.

The imperative for human freedom at the core of American foreign policy for most of the twentieth century, and likewise at the core of the Exodus experience, has been given an enormous boost in the past few years with the remarkable changes in Eastern Europe and the Soviet Union, as they throw off the twentieth century yoke of Communist oppression.

We recognize at Passover, more than any other time during the year, the essential unity of the Jewish experience; that no Jew can feel totally free while other Jews lack the freedom to practice their faith wherever they wish. It underscores for us that we must never again acquiesce while other Jews are threatened, as too many American Jews did during World War II.

This new Haggadah demonstrates in picture and word how American Jews have looked upon Passover over the generations and incorporated its meaning into their lives. As no other Haggadah, it captures the spirit of Passover in America and its importance to Jewish continuity.

But for me, the American Heritage Haggadah is not only a joy to read and a welcome education in American and Jewish history; it offers a badly needed challenge as we look at the future of American Jewry into the twenty-first century.

The freedom that Passover stresses was not intended to be freedom without responsibility. The liberation from Egypt was quickly followed by the responsibilities at Mt Sinai. We American Jews in recent years have too often abused the unprecedented freedom to practice our religion that the United States affords by abandoning Judaism entirely and melting into the general American landscape. Indeed, our greatest challenge is not our ancient external enemy of antisemitism but the internal enemy of assimilation.

The problem is that a large part of the Jewish community is abandoning its Jewish roots, exercising the freedom of choice America provides by neglecting its responsibilities to Judaism. We can no longer deny the potentially dire implication of recent trends in the Jewish community.

By so wonderfully integrating American history and Passover observance in the American Heritage Haggadah, the publishers have graphically reminded us that we can be both good Americans and good Jews; that America has never demanded assimilation as a price of acceptance; that we add most to the rich mosaic of America by strengthening our Jewish ties, not neglecting them. The American Heritage Haggadah will prove to be a timeless Haggadah with a timeless — and timely — message.

Stuart E. Eizenstat
Washington D.C.
Hanukka 5752
December 1991

Stuart E. Eizenstat was the domestic policy adviser to President Jimmy Carter. He is an attorney practising in Washington D.C. and is a leading advocate for the intensification of Jewish education in the USA.

Supporters of the American Heritage Haggadah

Mr. and Mrs. George Alterman
Mr. and Mrs. Paul Baker
Judge and Mrs. Bernard Balick
Mr. and Mrs. Oscar B. Birshtein
Mr. and Mrs. Frank Chaiken
Mr. and Mrs. Eli Evans
Mr. and Mrs. Stephen D. Gardner
Mr. and Mrs. Louis Geffen
Mrs. Miriam Gibstein
Mrs. Helen Goldstein
Mr. and Mrs. Jack Horowitz
Mr. and Mrs. Richard Kane
Judge and Mrs. Charles Keil
Mr. and Mrs. Joel Kopler
Mr. and Mrs. Richard Longwill
Mr. Paul Mansbach
Rabbi and Mrs. Arthur Oleisky
Prof. and Mrs. Albert Potts
The Raskas family
Mr. and Mrs. Herbert Richman
Mr. and Mrs. Allan Rinzler
Mr. and Mrs. Harry Sander
Mr. and Mrs. Dov Schlein
Mr. and Mrs. Bernard Siegel
Mr. and Mrs. Stuart Weitzman
Simon Family Fund

Atlanta Jewish Federation
Rabbi Jacob Kraft Educational Foundation
of Congregation Beth Shalom
Nomis Philanthropic Fund

In loving memory of
Mrs. Lottie Geffen Simon
Mr. Abraham Simon
Harold William Simon
Mr. Samuel Joseph Birshtein
Mr. Mayer Isaac (Easy) Birshtein

Acknowledgements

$\mathcal{A}$ project of the dimensions of the American Heritage Haggadah required a great deal of assistance and encouragement.

My publishers, Ilan and Dror Greenfield, had a personal interest in the Haggadah throughout its development, devoting unlimited time and energy to insure its uniqueness.

Gila Nidam of Gefen Publishing House worked untold hours in designing this Haggadah. Its distinctiveness results from the way in which she took the individual components and fashioned a visually exciting volume.

Ezra Gorodesky and Rafi Grafman, fellow Jerusalemites, loaned me primary source material and shared their expertise graciously while I was working on the Haggadah. I am forever indebted to them, and I want to thank them publicly for the Judaica which they have preserved.

A treasured friend and noted anthologist, Rabbi Philip Goodman, shared with me his personal knowledge of American Jewish history, life and culture thereby opening channels of inquiry which I might never have entered.

Two eminent Haggadah collectors, Moshe Yaari of Jerusalem and Stephen Durchslag of Chicago, opened their collections to me. What a treat to peruse personally so many American Haggadot from 1837 to the present.

My cousin, Professor Dov Levin, has always taken a special interest in my work, and he particularly urged me to see this project through to fruition.

My mentor, the dean of American Jewish historians, Professor Jacob Rader Marcus of the Hebrew Union College-Jewish Institute of Religion, has always responded to my questions with his encyclopedic knowledge of American Jewish history.

At the National Library in Jerusalem, I discovered a treasure trove of source material on Passover in the U.S.A. The staff in the Judaica reading room there did not always appreciate the many books of all sizes, which I kept on reserve, but they helped me unstintingly. Albert in the photographic services division made wonderful reproductions of the items used from the library's holdings.

My special thanks to the staff at the American Jewish Historical Society, American Jewish Archives, Western Jewish History Center of the Judah L. Magnes Museum, YIVO, Congregation Beth Elohim, Charleston, South Carolina, Judaica Division of the Library of Congress, Judaica Collection of the Widener Library, Harvard University, Special Collections division of the Woodruff Library, Emory University, Jewish Museum and to my colleagues and friends in Israel and the U.S.A. for their assistance and for the materials they loaned for inclusion in the Haggadah.

Finally, I want to thank Eli Evans, president of the Revson Foundation, a fellow southerner and a leading figure in the development of American Jewish life. He immediately empathized with my quest, urging me to complete this Haggadah. His personal assistance helped insure the appearance of this volume.

D.G.

XIII

Haggadah for Passover ed. J.D. Eisenstein, New York, 1920

Baking for Passover with matzah meal, *HaDoar* Hebrew Weekly, NewYork, 1932

Passover Eve On the East Side

Preparations for Passover

New York, April, 1905

XV

The Preparation and Sale of Matzah

Frank Leslie's Illustrated Newspaper April 10, 1858

Ezra P. Gorodesky Collection

The rabbi checks the flour before the matzah dough is prepared

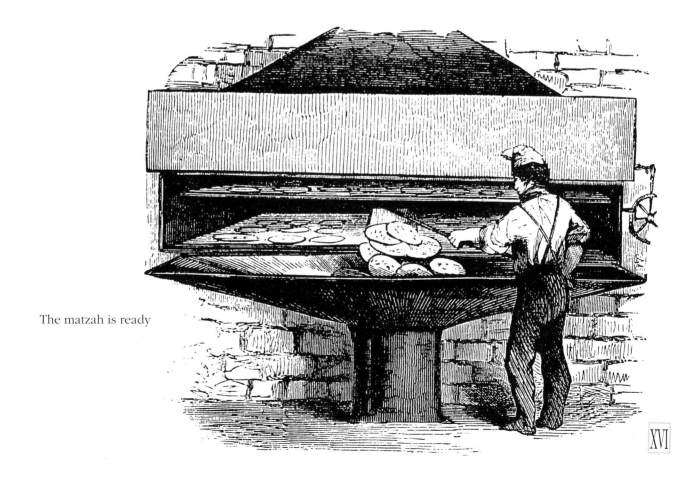

The matzah is ready

Grinding the matzah meal

The sale at Mark Isaacs' store on Division Street in New York City

Passover greetings from the Bronx
distributor of Dr. Brown's soda.
Der Tag (daily Yiddish newspaper),
New York, March 17, 1924

New York, April, 1935

PASSOVER CRUISE

Dietary Laws may be observed on the

S. S. AQUITANIA
(CUNARD LINE)

Sailing April 22nd

4 Days to Bermuda $50 up

Leblang Travel Bureau

S. E. Cor. 43d St. and B'way

Entrance thru GRAY'S

Tel. BRyant 9-2621-2622

Clothes for the Holidays

The Right Style for Passover
The Jewish Criterion, Pittsburgh,
Pennsylvania,
April 8, 1921

Congressman
Herbert
Tenzer sells his
"chometz" in
1965.
*American Jewish
Historical Society*,
Waltham,
Massachusetts

Checking the matzah
before it is boxed,
New York, 1951

XVIII

The George Washington Seder -1889

The centennial of the inauguration of George Washington, the first president of the United States, was marked in April 1889 with great pageantry and grand celebrations. Since the actual anniversary of the inauguration fell during Passover that year, American Jews chose to use their homes in general and the seder in particular as the focus for the celebration of this event.

A month before Passover it was announced in New York that a free picture of George Washington would be given with every ten pounds of matzah purchased. Rabbi Jacob Joseph, the chief rabbi of New York, composed a prayer for the occasion which was to be read in all synagogues during Passover. Across the United States, synagogue buildings were decorated with red, white and blue bunting to capture the spirit of the centennial.

The illustration by Arthur Meyer from *The American Hebrew* newspaper on April 19, 1889, dramatizes what many Jewish homes looked like for the seder that year. Prominently displayed near the front door was the picture of George Washington so that Elijah could be welcomed by America's first president. The champion of American independence and the first president to have contact with the Jews in the United States, Washington was naturally woven into the Jewish celebration of freedom.

בְּדִיקַת חָמֵץ·

אוֹר לְי״ד בְּנִיסָן וּכְשֶׁחָל י״ד בְּשַׁבָּת אוֹר לְי״ג, בּוֹדְקִין אֶת הֶחָמֵץ לְאוֹר הַנֵּר סְיד אַחַר ת״ע. וְקוֹדֶם הַבְּדִיקָה יְבָרֵךְ.

בָּרוּךְ אַתָּה יְיָ אֱלֹהֵינוּ מֶלֶךְ הָעוֹלָם אֲשֶׁר קִדְּשָׁנוּ בְּמִצְוֹתָיו וְצִוָּנוּ עַל בִּעוּר חָמֵץ:

סְיד אַחַר הַבְּדִיקָה יְבַטֵל כָל חָמֵץ שֶׁבִּרְשׁוּתוֹ הַבִּלְתִּי יָדוּעַ לוֹ שֶׁמָא כָעָלָם מִמֶּנּוּ, וְיֹאמַר:

כָּל חֲמִירָא וַחֲמִיעָא דְּאִכָּא בִרְשׁוּתִי דְּלָא חֲמִתֵּהּ וְדְלָא בַעַרְתֵּהּ לִבְטִיל וְלֶהֱוֵי כְּעַפְרָא דְאַרְעָא:

הֶחָמֵץ שֶׁמָּצָא כּוֹהֲנִים לְשָׁמְרוּ עַד שְׁעַת הַבִּעוּר וְלִשְׂרְפוּ נע״פ בַּתְחִלָּת שָׁעָה שָׁשִׁית, וְעַכְשָׁו כֹהֲנוּ לְשָׂרְפוּ בַּסוֹף חֲמִישִׁית, וּבַבְטֵלִין פַּעַס שָׁנִית וְאוֹמְרִין כָּל חֲמִירָא וְכוּ׳ וְהַבָּטוֹל וְדְאִי שׁל״ל דּוֹקָא קוֹדֶם שָׁשִׁית לְפִי שֶׁאַחַר זְמַן אֲסוּרוֹ אִינוֹ בִרְשׁוּתוֹ לְבַטְּלוֹ.

כָּל חֲמִירָא וַחֲמִיעָא דְּאִכָּא בִרְשׁוּתִי דַחֲמִתֵּהּ וְדְלָא חֲמִתֵּהּ דְּבַעַרְתֵּהּ וְדְלָא בַעַרְתֵּהּ לִבְטִיל וְלֶהֱוֵי כְּעַפְרָא דְאַרְעָא:

This illustration drawn in Chicago, Illinois, in the late 1870s,
is the earliest American depiction of the search for leaven. The turbaned
father plans to collect the pieces of bread in the wooden spoon
which he is holding. However, neither a feather nor a brush normally
used in the ceremony is visible.
Haggadah for Passover ed. Hayyim Liberman, Chicago,1879

On a dock in Bahrain, American
soldiers burn the leaven collected from
the Cunard Princess ship the night
before - March 29, 1991.
David Zalis Collection

Searching for Leaven - 1879

The searching shall be done in this
manner: the master of the house shall
order all the rooms to be cleanly
swept. One of the family shall put a
few crumbs of bread on different
places thereof. And then by the light
of a candle, he shall thoroughly
examine and search every corner.
After he is through with the searching,
he should then carefully lay away the
food which he intends to use before
Passover and take particular care that
no cats or rats have access to it, for
should any of the leavened food be
moved from its place by some
unknown object, he will have to
re-examine the premises.
The next morning, at eleven, these
crumbs of leavened bread are
publicly burned.
If there is any particular sale of
chametz to a Gentile, it must be
conducted in a manner agreeable to
the laws of the country.
Haggadah for Passover
ed. Hayyim Liberman, Chicago, 1879

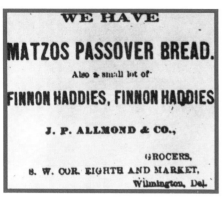

WE HAVE
MATZOS PASSOVER BREAD.
Also a small lot of
FINNON HADDIES, FINNON HADDIES
J. P. ALLMOND & CO.,
GROCERS,
S. W. COR. EIGHTH AND MARKET,
Wilmington, Del.

In 1881 J.P. Allmond, the mayor of Wilmington, Delaware, had Passover staples for sale at his store. It is not clear whether finnan haddies, a type of fish, were kosher for Passover. *Every Evening*, Wilmington, Delaware, March 18,1881.

Haggadah for Passover ed. J.D. Eisenstein, New York 1920. Art Lola.

Removing the Leaven

On the night before Passover Eve, immediately after the Maariv evening service, all the leaven in the home is searched out and collected. To make sure that the blessing is not said in vain, a few pieces, usually 10, are placed in various parts of the house and searched out. Before the search, light a candle and say the following blessing:

Be blessed, God, our god, King of the universe, Who has sanctified us by His commandments and commanded us concerning the removal of leaven.

After the search say:

Let any leaven within the precincts of my home, even if I may not have seen and removed it, be considered null and void and as public property, like the dust of the earth.

On the following morning burn the leaven and say:

Let any leaven within the precincts of my home, whether I have seen it or not, whether I have removed it or not, be considered null and void and as public property, like the dust of the earth.

Removing the Leaven from our Lives and our Hearts

Last Passover we took from our homes the leaven, and doubtless most of us resolved to take it from our hearts. The words of the rabbi had impressed us; he had awakened old memories, recalled broken resolutions, and even as he spoke the ferment of the leaven went on within us. How this same old leaven had time and again bothered us, but this time we intended to make sure that the chometz had left our lives. Our temporal abode might realize the high destiny for which it has been ordained. Our suffering brothers learn how near at heart we have their weal or woe. The troubled should find us with a ready ear and responsive voice and hand. Our children should know that to be a Jew is to be the ideal creature of mankind and the real man of God. . .Our children however, are deaf to our prayers, adamant to our persuasions, but we have been likewise. It has been business, business, all the year round, how much we could earn, how much we could save. The hour that will not return us so much of the coin of the country is to us an hour lost. On one side of the earth millions are in bondage to a despotic tyrant, fettered hand and foot, but still soul free, loyal in spirit, as loyalty is understood. Here in America, thousands are in soul slavery, bound body and spirit to business; understanding their duty, but deliberately neglecting it. And is this the way we are preparing for our grand mission?

Ray Frank
Passover sermon 1894

Ray Frank (1864-1948) was among the first women to preach in an American synagogue, when she addressed a congregation in Spokane, Washington in 1890.

American Jewish Historical Society
Waltham, Massachusetts

The noted anthologist, Rabbi Philip Goodman, shown second from the right, conducted a seder in 1942 at Camp Upton, Long Island, New York. In attendance were more than 200 new U.S. Army recruits. Behind the head table is a "V" for victory made out of matzah.

Philip Goodman collection

The Seder-leader arranges the symbols on the tray, explaining as he does so. First, he puts three matzot on the tray, usually inside a specially designed cloth with three pockets.

The Zero'a — a small piece of roast, — is put at the top right. This is in remembrance of the Passover Offering sacrificed in the Temple. At the top left a roasted egg is placed, in remembrance of the Hagigah (Festival) offering sacrificed in the Temple.

In the center, just below the zero'a and the egg, the marror — bitter herbs — is placed.

The Haroset is placed at the bottom right. To soften the bitterness of the marror it is dipped in the Haroset concoction whose basic ingredients are usually ground apples, almonds and dates, cinnamon, ginger and sweet wine or liqueur, made to a thick consistency to resemble the clay from which our ancestors in Egypt had to make bricks.

The Karpas vegetable — greens or a boiled potato — is placed at the bottom-left.

Below the Haroset and karpas, and in line with the marror, the hazeret is placed. This, too, is a bitter herb, usually a horseradish root, and is used for the Korech sandwich eaten just before the meal begins.

An "Elijah's Winecup" is displayed in the center of the table, for use later in the Seder, in anticipation of Prophet Elijah, who is to announce the coming of the Messiah.

Seder plate depicted on a matzah cover. Geffen family collection, Woodruff Memorial Library Special Collections, Emory University

4

The Seder

Person conducting the Seder opens with the following explanation of the order — which is what the Hebrew word "seder" means — of the Passover night service.

קַדֵּשׁ **KADESH:** Inaugurate the festival over wine

וּרְחַץ **U'REHATZ:** Rinse the hands without saying the blessing

כַּרְפַּס **KARPAS:** Eat vegetables dipped in salt water or vinegar

יַחַץ **YAHATZ:** Split the middle matzah

מַגִּיד **MAGGID:** Recite the Haggada

רָחְצָה **RAHATZA:** Rinse the hands and say the blessing

מוֹצִיא **MOTZI:** Say the bread blessing

מַצָּה **MATZAH:** Say the matzah blessing

מָרוֹר **MAROR:** Eat bitter herb

כּוֹרֵךְ **KORECH:** Eat bitter herb sandwich

שֻׁלְחָן עוֹרֵךְ **SHULHAN ORECH:** Eat the festival meal

צָפוּן **TZAFUN:** Eat the afikoman

בָּרֵךְ **BARECH:** Say the Grace-after-Meals

הַלֵּל **HALLEL:** Chant the "Hallel" praise and thanksgiving Psalms

נִרְצָה **NIRTZA:** Pray that God accept our service and prayer

קַדֵּשׁ

נשבת מתחילין כאן :

בלחש ויהי ערב ויהי בקר נקול יום הַשִּׁשִּׁי : וַיְכֻלּוּ הַשָּׁמַיִם וְהָאָרֶץ וְכָל צְבָאָם : וַיְכַל אֱלֹהִים בַּיּוֹם הַשְּׁבִיעִי מְלַאכְתּוֹ אֲשֶׁר עָשָׂה וַיִּשְׁבּוֹת בַּיּוֹם הַשְּׁבִיעִי מִכָּל מְלַאכְתּוֹ אֲשֶׁר עָשָׂה : וַיְבָרֶךְ אֱלֹהִים אֶת יוֹם הַשְּׁבִיעִי וַיְקַדֵּשׁ אוֹתוֹ כִּי בוֹ שָׁבַת מִכָּל מְלַאכְתּוֹ אֲשֶׁר בָּרָא אֱלֹהִים לַעֲשׂוֹת :

נקול או במולאי שבת מתחילין כאן :

סַבְרִי מָרָנָן וְרַבָּנָן וְרַבּוֹתַי,

בָּרוּךְ אַתָּה יְיָ אֱלֹהֵינוּ מֶלֶךְ
הָעוֹלָם בּוֹרֵא פְּרִי הַגָּפֶן :

בָּרוּךְ אַתָּה יְיָ אֱלֹהֵינוּ מֶלֶךְ הָעוֹלָם אֲשֶׁר
בָּחַר בָּנוּ מִכָּל עָם וְרוֹמְמָנוּ מִכָּל לָשׁוֹן וְקִדְּשָׁנוּ
בְּמִצְוֹתָיו • וַתִּתֶּן לָנוּ יְיָ אֱלֹהֵינוּ בְּאַהֲבָה שבתות
למנוחה ומועדים לְשִׂמְחָה חַגִּים וּזְמַנִּים לְשָׁשׂוֹן
אֶת יוֹם השבת הזה ואת יום חַג הַמַּצּוֹת הַזֶּה •
זְמַן חֵרוּתֵנוּ באהבה מִקְרָא קֹדֶשׁ זֵכֶר לִיצִיאַת
מִצְרָיִם • כִּי בָּנוּ בָחַרְתָּ וְאוֹתָנוּ קִדַּשְׁתָּ מִכָּל
הָעַמִּים ושבת ומוֹעֲדֵי קָדְשֶׁךָ באהבה וברצון
בְּשִׂמְחָה וּבְשָׂשׂוֹן הִנְחַלְתָּנוּ בָּרוּךְ אַתָּה יְיָ
מְקַדֵּשׁ השבת וְיִשְׂרָאֵל וְהַזְּמַנִּים :

The Seder

Set the table in its proper order, let the youngest ask the questions and follow the prescribed ritual; chant the sing-song of the *Hagadah* to the end of *Chad Gadya*. What a supreme childishness! You can hear better music at the opera, more lively rhymes at the vaudeville. You can obtain more toothsome food than the *Matzo*, and the preservers of comestibles prepare nicer things than the bitter herbs and the saline dipped parsley and the chopped *Charoseth*.

Part of a generation has sneered at the old rite; part of a generation would forget it; part of a generation ignores, and the whole the self denial of the festival with its limitations to things unleavened; part of a generation, the largest of all, clings to it with intense determination.

The latter part is the true Israel, the banner bearer of our nation, whose strength has carried us through the ages, whose loyalty to tradition, keeps Israel in serried ranks — an army equipped to meet its destiny, an army that, marching now to a tune of sorrow, shall quicken its pace when the song of hope is sounded and shall effect that rush which the final onslaught to victory shall demand. It is not for nothing that the anthem of the service begs God to rebuild the Temple and the final passage tells of the Redemption of Humanity. Yes, to each and every element in our generation the *Seder* has its message, if only men would preach it instead of administering soporific homilies and conjuring moralities out of the various aspects of leaven and unleavened. Such cheap plausibilities do not move our age. The sermons in stones are read by everyone, and rejected — as stones.

The Maccabaean, monthly Journal of
Federation of American Zionists
ed. Jacob De Haas, April 1903

The Hebrew,
San Francisco,
April 1875

Mordecai Manuel Noah (1785-1851), a well-known personality in the USA before the Civil War, stated that only unfermented wine could be used on Passover. Thus, his 1846 raisin wine recipe was hailed by American temperance advocates.

Noah's Passover Raisin Wine Recipe - 1846

Take a gallon demijohn, or stone jug; pick three or four pounds of bloom raisins, break off the stems; put the raisins into the demijohn, and fill it with water. Tie a rag over the mouth, and place the demijohn near the fire, or on one side of the fire-place, to keep it warm. In about a week it wil be fit for use, making a pure, pleasant and sweet wine, free from alcohol. It may last from Sunday to Sunday without getting sour or tart; but it is easy to make a small quantity of wine for each time it is to be used. This is the wine we use on the nights of Passover.

Get the Thin Matzah

Dear Rebecca,

You had better begin to make all the preparations you can for Pesach. Don't buy anything more on the occasion than is absolutely necessary. It will be time enough next week to get our matsos. You may order them from the Dutch or Portugeese Congregation. I like the thin ones of last year but still I don't think there is as much substance in them as in those baked by our congregation. We want 100 lb besides whatever ground matsos you may require all put up in a new bundle tight.

Mordecai Manuel Noah
29 March 1846

Kadesh

Pour the first cup, everybody stands, recite the Kiddush holding the cup in the up-raised palm of the right hand.

(On Friday night begin here)

And there was evening and there was morning, the sixth day (Genesis 1:31) Heaven and earth were completed, and their entire host. On the seventh day God completed all the work He had been doing. and God blessed the seventh day and declared it holy, because on it He desisted from all the work of creation He had done (Genesis 2:1-3)

(On weekday nights begin here)

By your leave, masters, teachers and gentlemen:
Be blessed God, our god, King of the universe, Creator of the fruit of the vine.

(The passages in parentheses are said only on Friday night)

Be blessed, God, our god, King of the universe, Who chose us out of all the peoples, exalted us above all tongues, and sanctified us by His commandments. And lovingly You gave us, God, our god, (Sabbaths for rest and) set times for celebration, festivals and occasions for rejoicing, this (Sabbath day and this) Matzot Festival, and this holiday, this holy convocation, the occasion of our liberation (with love): a holy convocation in remembrance of the Exodus from Egypt. Indeed, You chose us and sanctified us from among all the peoples, (and Sabbaths) and Your holy set-times (lovingly and gladly,) happily and joyously did You bequeath to us. Be blessed, God, Who sanctifies (the Sabbath and) Israel and the festivals.

In this seder illustration from an American Yiddish textbook, even the babe in arms is present. Hebrew Publishing Company *New York, 1929*

בָּרוּךְ אַתָּה יְיָ אֱלֹהֵינוּ מֶלֶךְ הָעוֹלָם בּוֹרֵא מְאוֹרֵי הָאֵשׁ :
בָּרוּךְ אַתָּה יְיָ אֱלֹהֵינוּ מֶלֶךְ הָעוֹלָם הַמַּבְדִּיל בֵּין קֹדֶשׁ
לְחוֹל בֵּין אוֹר לְחֹשֶׁךְ בֵּין יִשְׂרָאֵל לָעַמִּים . בֵּין יוֹם הַשְּׁבִיעִי
לְשֵׁשֶׁת יְמֵי הַמַּעֲשֶׂה . בֵּין קְדֻשַּׁת שַׁבָּת לִקְדֻשַּׁת יוֹם טוֹב
הִבְדַּלְתָּ . וְאֶת יוֹם הַשְּׁבִיעִי מִשֵּׁשֶׁת יְמֵי הַמַּעֲשֶׂה קִדַּשְׁתָּ .
הִבְדַּלְתָּ וְקִדַּשְׁתָּ אֶת עַמְּךָ יִשְׂרָאֵל בִּקְדֻשָּׁתֶךָ . בָּרוּךְ
אַתָּה יְיָ הַמַּבְדִּיל בֵּין קֹדֶשׁ לְקֹדֶשׁ :

בָּרוּךְ אַתָּה יְיָ אֱלֹהֵינוּ מֶלֶךְ הָעוֹלָם
שֶׁהֶחֱיָנוּ וְקִיְּמָנוּ וְהִגִּיעָנוּ לַזְּמַן הַזֶּה :

How to Lean on Passover

Then, instead of appearing in the posture of a traveller, he leans, in a stately manner, his left arm on a couch, or bed, made up for the occasion, as an indication of the liberty and the rest which the Israelites regained when they departed Egypt, and drinks of the first cup, in which he is followed by all the company.

The Passover,
Brooklyn 1830, p.15.

Signs of the 1920s in America can be discerned by the feminine hairdos and the boy's cap. A pitcher is carried to the table so that everyone can wash their hands at their seat.
Haggadah for Passover

Hebrew Publishing Company, 1921

Dear Sister!
We have kosher meat, a burial ground, and a synagogue which was formed three days before Passover, by 12 single young men and one married man. We have now 42 members principally English, and we have some old married men to lead us the correct way. Our form of prayers is that of the Great Synagogue. We voted in our officers, who are all married men except two. I was elected honorary secretary, and had 38 out of 42 votes. There was a congregation formed last year but they could not agree; they have, however, again formed themselves into a congregation and number 60 members, German, Portugese and Americans, but it is not supposed it will last long. Ours is considered the correct congregation, as we have a shochet, but for which office they have no competent person. Our president is Mr. Joseph, an American, our treasurer, Mr. Hart, a Pole. Mr. Isaacs of Brown's has baked the matzos for Passover with whom 12 of us youngsters passed the festival. I do not think that the Jews in any part of the world could have kept the Passover more strictly than we did.

S.H. Cohen

Jewish Chronicle,
London, July 18, 1851

If the Seder takes place on Saturday night,
add the following two blessings:

Be blessed, God, our god, King of the universe, creator of the firelights.

Be blessed, God, our god, King of the universe, Who distinguishes between the holy and the commonplace, between light and darkness, between Israel and the other peoples, between the seventh day and the six workdays. You have distinguished between the sanctity of the Sabbath and holiday sanctity, and the seventh day You declared holy above the six workdays. You set apart and hallowed Your people, Israel, with Your holiness. Be blessed, God, Who distinguishes between one sanctity and another sanctity.

The following blessing is always said:

Be blessed, God, our god, King of the universe, for keeping us alive, and sustaining us, and enabling us to reach this occasion.

The First American Seder Drawing

This seder scene is part of a large drawing entitled "The Rites and Worship of the Israelites," executed in 1859 in New York. A small book, by Cantor Max Wolff of New York, accompanied and explained each section of the drawing. At this pre-Civil War seder, the father wears his high hat, reminiscent of the religious German Jews who had migrated to America. The child sits in a highchair, prevalent in the USA at that period. The Hebrew is written by hand and seems amateurish. The mantlepiece was a common feature in American homes.

Collection of Beth Elohim Congregation,
Charleston, South Carolina

Even the Neediest on Skid Row Were Invited to a Seder

Phillip McLachian, a 23-year-old ex-felon and recovering drug user, learned a new word on Sunday, Dayenu, which in Hebrew means "enough."

McLachian was one of 50 clients of the Skid Row-based Weingart Center who participated in their first Passover seder, held by Los Angeles Jewish Family Services and B'nai B'rith. They were joined by about 40 Jewish senior citizens from the Israel Levin Center in Venice.

Each year, they have invited both a Jewish cantor and a Protestant pastor to preside.

"This is the only ecumenical seder in the city," Sara Glazer, the coordinator said. "The key word is freedom. That is the story of the Jewish people and it is the story of very many other people, like those here today."

Jervis Reed, a former kindergarten teacher who had been hooked on rock cocaine, said the seder was more than just an unusual meal.

"I feel maybe I can relate more to a Jewish person now than I could before," Reed said. "Maybe we would have something to talk about."

Los Angeles Times
April 24, 1989

וְרַחַץ וְשׁוֹתִין בַּהֲסִבַּת שְׂמֹאל וְאח"כ נוֹטֵל יָדָיו וְלֹא יְבָרֵךְ נְטִילָה.

כַּרְפַּס וְיִקַּח אִיסוּף שֶׁהוּא פִּיטְרוֹזִיל אוֹ קִירְבִיל שֶׁהוּא כַרְפַּס. מְעַט וְלֹא קַלַח. וְיִטְבּוֹל בַּחוֹמֶץ אוֹ בְּמֵי מֶלַח. וִיבָרֵךְ :

בָּרוּךְ אַתָּה יְיָ אֱלֹהֵינוּ מֶלֶךְ הָעוֹלָם בּוֹרֵא פְּרִי הָאֲדָמָה :

יַחַץ יִקַּח הַמַּצָה אֶמְצָעִי וְיִבְצָעֶנָּה לְשְׁנַיִם. בְּלִי עֲלָלָתִים. הַחֵלֶק הַגָּדוֹל בֵּין כָּר לַכַּסָּה תַּחַת מַרְאֲשׁוֹתָיו יִטְמִין. לְעֵסֶק תְּהֵי שְׁמוּרָה לַאֲפִיקוֹמֶן. וּפְרוּסָה הַקְּטַנָּה הַשְּׁבוּרָה. תָּשִׂים עַל מְקוֹמָה בַּקְּעָרָה :

מַגִּיד מַגְבִּיהַּ הַקְּעָרָה. וְה"כ תַּנְמִילִין נְתַּחִילָה לְהַסֵּב. נַסְּעָה שָׁאוֹמֵר כַּהֲדָא לַחֲמָא נָקוֹל רַס :

הָא לַחְמָא עַנְיָא דִּי אֲכָלוּ אַבְהָתָנָא בְּאַרְעָא דְמִצְרָיִם · כָּל דִּכְפִין יֵיתֵי וְיֵכֹל · כָּל דִּצְרִיךְ יֵיתֵי וְיִפְסַח · הָשַׁתָּא הָכָא · לְשָׁנָה הַבָּאָה בְּאַרְעָא דְיִשְׂרָאֵל · הָשַׁתָּא עַבְדֵי · לְשָׁנָה הַבָּאָה בְּנֵי חוֹרִין :

Drink the first cup, reclining.

U'rehatz — Rinse the hands without saying the blessing.

Karpas — Dip vegetable in salt water or vinegar and say the following blessing before eating:

Be blessed, God, our god, King of the universe, Creator of the fruit of the soil.

Yahatz — Split the middle matzah; leave the smaller piece in its place between two whole matzot and wrap the larger piece in a napkin for the Afikoman.

Maggid — Begin reciting the Haggada by saying:

Yesterday we were slaves, today we are free.
In urgent haste we departed from Egypt.

Lift the Seder tray and say:

This is the poverty bread that our ancestors ate in Egypt. Let anyone who is hungry enter and eat; let anyone who is needy enter and join us in our Passover feast. This year we are here; next year may we be in the Land of Israel. This year we are slaves; next year may we be free people.

The Matzah of Unity

We are about to take the middle matzah and divide it in half. This matzah which we break and set aside is a symbol of our unity with the Jews of the Soviet Union. We will not conclude our Seder until the missing piece is found and spiritually reunited. This reminds us of the indestructible link which unifies us as a world family.

Matzah is the bread of affliction which after the Exodus becomes the bread of redemption. As we observe this festival of freedom, we are heartened to be part of the largest Exodus of Soviet Jews in recent history, but we remain mindful of those refuseniks who still wait longingly for permission to emigrate.

Jews of the Soviet Union resisted decades of suppression with faith. Struggling to live as Jews, many sought valiantly to leave for Israel, the land of our redemption. Many suffered harassment; some endured prison. The forces of oppression tried to afflict them with amnesia of the spirit. But, they remembered.

At last, most are allowed to go free. We know not how long the door of freedom will remain open. We walk with them in their Exodus. At this Seder, we commit ourselves to accompany them on their road to freedom, pledging the assistance they require.

We cannot forget those who remain behind. To those still seeking permission to leave and to those striving to build a better Jewish life in the Soviet Union, we pledge our continued vigilance, self-sacrifice and solidarity.

Later, we will search for the hidden piece of matzah. In the same way, we have sought to find our brothers and sisters in the Soviet Union. Once having found the missing half, we will be able to continue our Seder. So, too, will the reunification of Soviet Jews with our homeland allow Israel to continue growing and blossoming into the central core of our collective Jewish identity. May our commitment, expressed here tonight as well as maintained through Operation Exodus Tomorrow, enhance the quality of Soviet Jewish life in Israel.
Am Israel Hu Am Echad - The People Of Israel Are United.

Prepared by the United Jewish Appeal Rabbinic Cabinet and the National Conference on Soviet Jewry in honor of Operation Exodus-Pesach 5750-Passover 1990.

Moscow Seder
"Unity Sedarim" in Washington, Jerusalem, Moscow marked Operation Exodus in April 1990.

Маца Единства

Евреи Советского Союза десятилетиями сопротивлялись подавлению их прав, но не теряли надежду. В борьбе за свое стремление жить как евреи, многие героически пытались выехать в Израиль – страну нашего освобождения. Многие пострадали, оказались в тюрьмах. Силы деспотизма и угнетения старались поразить их болезнью духовного забвения. Но они помнили!

מַצַת הָאַחְדוּת

סוֹף סוֹף, רוּבָּם הִרְשׁוּ לָצֵאת כְּמָה זְמַן תִּשָּׁאֵר הַדֶּלֶת לַחֵרוּת אֶל הַחוֹפְשׁ. אֵין צוֹעֲדִים אָנוּ לָדַעַת בִּיצִיאַת מִצְרַיִם שֶׁלָהֶם. בַּסֵדֶר הַזֶּה, אָנוּ מִתְחַיְבִים אָתָּם לְלַוֹותָם בְּדַרְכָּם לַחוֹפְשׁ, בְּהַבְטָחָה לְהַגִּישׁ אֶת הַסִיוּע הַדָּרוּשׁ לָהֶם.

עוֹקֵר הַקְּעָרָה מֵעַל הַשֻּׁלְחָן כְּשֶׁמַּתְחִיל מַה נִּשְׁתַּנָה. וּמוֹחֲזִין כּוֹס תְּבַיִינָא:

מַה נִּשְׁתַּנָּה הַלַּיְלָה הַזֶּה מִכָּל הַלֵּילוֹת· שֶׁבְּכָל הַלֵּילוֹת אָנוּ אוֹכְלִין חָמֵץ וּמַצָּה· הַלַּיְלָה הַזֶּה כֻּלּוֹ מַצָּה: שֶׁבְּכָל הַלֵּילוֹת אָנוּ אוֹכְלִין שְׁאָר יְרָקוֹת הַלַּיְלָה הַזֶּה מָרוֹר: שֶׁבְּכָל הַלֵּילוֹת אֵין אָנוּ מַטְבִּילִין אֲפִילוּ פַּעַם אֶחָת· הַלַּיְלָה הַזֶּה שְׁתֵּי פְעָמִים: שֶׁבְּכָל הַלֵּילוֹת אָנוּ אוֹכְלִין בֵּין יוֹשְׁבִין וּבֵין מְסֻבִּין· הַלַּיְלָה הַזֶּה כֻּלָּנוּ מְסֻבִּין:

A bob-haired young lady asks the first question about matzah and leavened bread.
Young Israel, Cincinnati, April 1925

HEBREW

שבכל הלילות .אנו אוכלין חמץ ומצה.
.הלילה הזה כלו מצה

Shebehcawl halehlot ahnew oaklean hametz ooh matza. Haliela hazeh coolow matza.

On all other nights we eat leavened bread and matzoh. On this night, we eat only matzoh.

YIDDISH

אלה נכאט פון אגאנץ יאר אסין מיר אלאלי
גריינצין· די נאכט פון פסח אסין מיר
נאר מרור:

Aleh necht fun a gantze yohr esen mir alehley greentzen. Diz nacht fun Pesach esen mir nor moror.

On all other nights we eat all kinds of herbs. On this night we eat mainly bitters.

LADINO

קי אין טודאס לאס נוג'יס נון נוס אינטי-
ניינטיס אפּיילו בּ'יז אונה. אי לה נוג'י לה
איסטה דוס בּ'זיס.

Que en todas las noches non nos entientes afilu ves una. Y la noche la esta dos vezes.

On all other nights we do not dip even once. On this night we dip twice.

RUSSIAN

Все ночи мы кушаем сидя и облокотившись
а в эту ночь-только облокотишись?

Vese nochee mi kooshayem ceedya e oblocotivshes. Ah ve ehtoo noch tolko oblocotivshes.

On all other nights we eat either sitting straight or reclining. On this night we all recline.

Using the Four Questions, Passover continues the theme of America as a "Melting Pot," even in our own generation.
Southern Israelite, Atlanta, Georgia, April 17, 1981

Replace the tray on the table, pour the second cup of wine, and the youngest participant asks:

Why is this night different from all nights?

Why, on all other nights, do we eat either unleavened bread or matzah, but tonight we eat only matzah?

Why, on all other nights, do we eat all kinds of vegetables, but tonight we make a special point of eating bitter herbs?

Why, on all other nights, do we not make a point of dipping at all, but tonight we make a point of dipping twice?

Why, on all other nights, do we eat either sitting up or reclining, but tonight we all make a point of reclining?

Theodor Herzl Listens to the Four Questions

At the seder, the youngest child asks the four questions while his parents, grandmother and sister listen intently. Theodor Herzl, founder of the Zionist movement, is displayed prominently in a wall portrait. His picture replaces that of the famous rabbis which are frequently found on the walls and emphasizes the family's commitment to Zionism. This illustration appeared in *Shaharut*, March 1920, a Hebrew monthly for youth issued in New York by the Jewish Youth Publishing Company.

13

עֲבָדִים הָיִינוּ לְפַרְעֹה בְּמִצְרָיִם· וַיּוֹצִיאֵנוּ יְיָ
אֱלֹהֵינוּ מִשָּׁם בְּיָד חֲזָקָה וּבִזְרוֹעַ נְטוּיָה· וְאִלּוּ
לֹא הוֹצִיא הַקָּדוֹשׁ בָּרוּךְ הוּא אֶת אֲבוֹתֵינוּ
מִמִּצְרַיִם הֲרֵי אָנוּ וּבָנֵינוּ וּבְנֵי בָנֵינוּ מְשֻׁעְבָּדִים
הָיִינוּ לְפַרְעֹה בְּמִצְרָיִם· וַאֲפִילוּ כֻּלָּנוּ חֲכָמִים·
כֻּלָּנוּ נְבוֹנִים· כֻּלָּנוּ זְקֵנִים· כֻּלָּנוּ יוֹדְעִים אֶת
הַתּוֹרָה· מִצְוָה עָלֵינוּ לְסַפֵּר בִּיצִיאַת מִצְרָיִם·
וְכָל הַמַּרְבֶּה לְסַפֵּר בִּיצִיאַת מִצְרַיִם הֲרֵי
זֶה מְשֻׁבָּח:

מַעֲשֶׂה בְּרַבִּי אֱלִיעֶזֶר וְרַבִּי יְהוֹשֻׁעַ וְרַבִּי
אֶלְעָזָר בֶּן עֲזַרְיָה וְרַבִּי עֲקִיבָא וְרַבִּי טַרְפוֹן
שֶׁהָיוּ מְסֻבִּין בִּבְנֵי בְרַק· וְהָיוּ מְסַפְּרִים בִּיצִיאַת
מִצְרַיִם כָּל אוֹתוֹ הַלַּיְלָה· עַד שֶׁבָּאוּ תַלְמִידֵיהֶם
וְאָמְרוּ לָהֶם רַבּוֹתֵינוּ הִגִּיעַ זְמַן קְרִיאַת שְׁמַע
שֶׁל שַׁחֲרִית:

אָמַר רַבִּי אֶלְעָזָר בֶּן עֲזַרְיָה· הֲרֵי אֲנִי כְּבֶן
שִׁבְעִים שָׁנָה· וְלֹא זָכִיתִי שֶׁתֵּאָמֵר יְצִיאַת
מִצְרַיִם בַּלֵּילוֹת· עַד שֶׁדְּרָשָׁהּ בֶּן זוֹמָא· שֶׁנֶּאֱמַר
לְמַעַן תִּזְכֹּר אֶת יוֹם צֵאתְךָ מֵאֶרֶץ מִצְרַיִם
כָּל יְמֵי חַיֶּיךָ: יְמֵי חַיֶּיךָ, הַיָּמִים· כָּל יְמֵי חַיֶּיךָ,
הַלֵּילוֹת· וַחֲכָמִים אוֹמְרִים יְמֵי חַיֶּיךָ, הָעוֹלָם
הַזֶּה· כָּל יְמֵי חַיֶּיךָ· לְהָבִיא לִימוֹת הַמָּשִׁיחַ:

The artist seeks to recall
the Haggadah text by depicting rabbis
dressed in second century C.E.
clothing. The drawing of Bnai Brak,
Eretz Yisrael, includes the typical
columns and buildings of that era.
Passover Haggadah, Shulsinger
Brothers, 1942. Art, Nota Koslowsky

**Not Only 70-year-olds but
100-year-olds Recount the Exodus**

Nissen Rosenstein, age 105, and Ettel
Polaski, 110 years old, will be seated at
the head of the seder table. They will
be participating in the seder at the
Home of Daughters of Jacob, 303 E.
Broadway. Present will be 195 people,
aged 110 to 67.

Six rabbis will be among the attendees
and will include Reuben Samuel
Supertinsky, 101, Jacob Margolis, 95,
and Mendel Lerner, the youngster
at 77.

New York Times,
March 29, 1915

The father expounds on the Exodus saga. The sons wear bowties, a form of dress common in post World War II years.
The Jewish Home,
New York, April 1950

Uncover the matzot and say:

We were Pharaoh's slaves in Egypt, and God, our god, took us out of there with a strong hand and outstretched arm. If the Blessed Holy One had not taken our ancestors out of Egypt, we, our children and our children's children would still be enslaved to Pharaoh in Egypt. And even if all of us were wise, even if all of us were clever, even if all of us were sages, even if all of us knew the Torah — we would still be duty bound to talk about the Exodus from Egypt. And the more you elaborate on the story of the Exodus from Egypt, the more praiseworthy you are.

It is told about Rabbi Eliezer, Rabbi Yehoshua, Rabbi Elazar son of Azaria, Rabbi Akiva and Rabbi Tarfon: One Passover night they were reclining together in Bnei Brak talking about the Exodus from Egypt. This went on all night, till their disciples came and said to them: "Masters, it is time to recite the morning Sh'ma.

Rabbi Elazar son of Azariah said: Here I am like 70 years old, yet I never understood why the story about the Exodus from Egypt should be recited at night, until Ben Zoma explained it on the basis of the verse (Deuteronomy 16:3), "So that you shall remember the day of your departure from Egypt all the days of your life." If it had been written "the days of your life," it would have meant the days only; but "all the days of your life" means the nights, too. The other Sages explain "all" to mean the Messianic Era, in addition to "the days of the present-time."

The Hard Week of Passover
Philadelphia, Pa.
April 11, 1813

Dear Maria,

I believe this is the very time a journey might be useful to you and if you can live with us through the hard week of Passover you may be assured of every other comfort friendship can prepare for your reception.

Rebecca Gratz

Rebecca Gratz (1781-1869) consecrated her life to the well-being and education of American Jews. It is suggested that she was the model for Rebecca in Sir Walter Scott's novel
Ivanhoe.

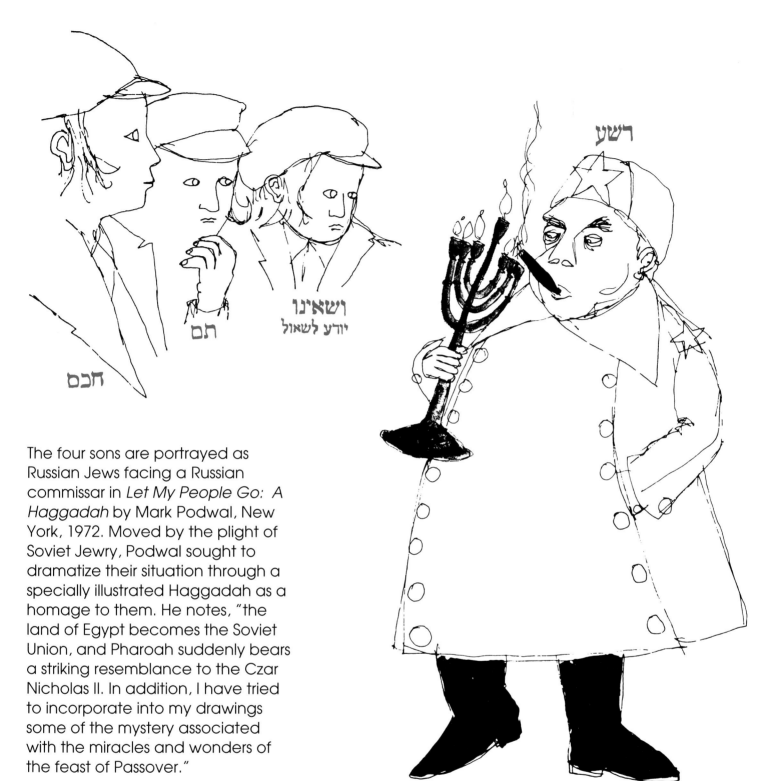

רשע

ושאינו
יודע לשאול

תם

חכם

The four sons are portrayed as Russian Jews facing a Russian commissar in *Let My People Go: A Haggadah* by Mark Podwal, New York, 1972. Moved by the plight of Soviet Jewry, Podwal sought to dramatize their situation through a specially illustrated Haggadah as a homage to them. He notes, "the land of Egypt becomes the Soviet Union, and Pharoah suddenly bears a striking resemblance to the Czar Nicholas II. In addition, I have tried to incorporate into my drawings some of the mystery associated with the miracles and wonders of the feast of Passover."

In an introduction to the Haggadah by the actor and musician Theodore Bikel, he wrote, "Dr. Podwal's illustrations relate to the plight of the Jews in the Soviet Union as the contemporary version of Jews smarting under the whip of the oppressor. . .they remind us of fresh wounds… Hopefully in the years to come, this Haggadah will be in use in Jewish homes with children seeing in these pictures only another chapter in the long Jewish history of suffering and deprivation - but a chapter of the past."

Used by permission of Dr. Mark Podwal

בָּרוּךְ הַמָּקוֹם בָּרוּךְ הוּא • בָּרוּךְ שֶׁנָּתַן תּוֹרָה לְעַמּוֹ יִשְׂרָאֵל • בָּרוּךְ הוּא: כְּנֶגֶד אַרְבָּעָה בָנִים דִּבְּרָה תוֹרָה • אֶחָד חָכָם • וְאֶחָד רָשָׁע • וְאֶחָד תָּם • וְאֶחָד שֶׁאֵינוֹ יוֹדֵעַ לִשְׁאוֹל:

First American depiction
of the four sons
The "wicked" son has his hand raised in a taunting fashion while puffing on his cigarette; the "wise" son is poring over the Haggadah. Both the "simple" son and the one who "does not know how to ask" have their backs to the reader. It is difficult to differentiate between the two. One rarely finds all four sons seated at the Passover seder table in Haggadah illustrations.

Haggadah for Passover,
ed. Hayyim Liberman, Chicago, 1879

Blessed is the Omnipresent, blessed is He; blessed is the One Who gave the Torah to His people Israel — may He be blessed.
The Torah has four sons in mind: the wise son; the wicked son; the simple son; and the son who does not know how to ask.

These 4 sons are found in a Haggadah for a model seder.

חָכָם מַה הוּא אוֹמֵר מָה הָעֵדֹת וְהַחֻקִּים
וְהַמִּשְׁפָּטִים אֲשֶׁר צִוָּה יְיָ אֱלֹהֵינוּ אֶתְכֶם: וְאַף
אַתָּה אֱמָר לוֹ כְּהִלְכוֹת הַפֶּסַח אֵין מַפְטִירִין
אַחַר הַפֶּסַח אֲפִיקוֹמָן:

רָשָׁע מַה הוּא אוֹמֵר מָה הָעֲבֹדָה הַזֹּאת
לָכֶם: לָכֶם וְלֹא לוֹ • וּלְפִי שֶׁהוֹצִיא אֶת עַצְמוֹ מִן
הַכְּלָל כָּפַר בְּעִקָּר • וְאַף אַתָּה הַקְהֵה אֶת שִׁנָּיו
וֶאֱמָר לוֹ בַּעֲבוּר זֶה עָשָׂה יְיָ לִי בְּצֵאתִי
מִמִּצְרָיִם • לִי וְלֹא לוֹ • אִלּוּ הָיָה שָׁם • לֹא הָיָה נִגְאָל:

תָּם מַה הוּא אוֹמֵר מַה זֹּאת וְאָמַרְתָּ אֵלָיו
בְּחֹזֶק יָד הוֹצִיאָנוּ יְיָ מִמִּצְרַיִם מִבֵּית עֲבָדִים:

וְשֶׁאֵינוֹ יוֹדֵעַ לִשְׁאוֹל אַתְּ פְּתַח לוֹ שֶׁנֶּאֱמַר
וְהִגַּדְתָּ לְבִנְךָ בַּיּוֹם הַהוּא לֵאמֹר בַּעֲבוּר זֶה
עָשָׂה יְיָ לִי בְּצֵאתִי מִמִּצְרָיִם:

Four Children

18

The "rashah," "wicked son," has pointed ears and fang-like teeth which suggest his demonic nature. The "tahm," simple son, sports the wide lapels of the stylish dresser of the early fifties. The son "who does not know how to ask" is now a "na'ar," a lad, who sucks his fingers and carries a doll to demonstrate his innocence.

The Jewish Home,
New York, April, 1950

What does the wise son say? "What is the meaning of the precepts, statutes and laws that God, our god, has commanded you?" (Deuteronomy 6:20) You are to tell him the rules of Passover: "It is forbidden to conclude the Passover meal by announcing: Now to the afikoman!" (Mishna Pessahim 10:8)

What does the wicked son say? "What is this service of yours?" (Exodus 12:26) Since he has said "of yours," thus excluding himself from the community of Jews, he has denied God. So you are to take the bite out of him by saying to him: "This commemorates what God did for me when I went out of Egypt!" (Exodus 13:8) — "for me," not for him: had he been there, he would not have been liberated.

What does the simple son say? "What is this?" (Exodus 13:14) You are to tell him: "It was by might of hand that God took us out of Egypt, out of the land of slavery." (Exodus 13:14)

As for the son who does not know how to ask — you start him off, for it is written (Exodus 13:8): "You shall tell your son on that day, saying: 'This commemorates what God did for me when I went out of Egypt'."

The wicked son has become
a prize fighter.
Haggadah for Passover
ed. J.D. Eisenstein New York, 1920. Art, Lola.

North Africa

New Guinea

Newfoundland

The Jewish Chaplain
New York, June 1944
Philip Goodman Collection

יָכוֹל מֵרֹאשׁ חֹדֶשׁ· תַּלְמוּד לוֹמַר בַּיּוֹם הַהוּא·
אִי בַּיּוֹם הַהוּא יָכוֹל מִבְּעוֹד יוֹם· תַּלְמוּד לוֹמַר
בַּעֲבוּר זֶה· בַּעֲבוּר זֶה לֹא אָמַרְתִּי אֶלָּא
בְּשָׁעָה שֶׁיֵּשׁ מַצָּה וּמָרוֹר מֻנָּחִים לְפָנֶיךָ:

מִתְּחִלָּה עוֹבְדֵי עֲבוֹדָה זָרָה הָיוּ אֲבוֹתֵינוּ
וְעַכְשָׁו קֵרְבָנוּ הַמָּקוֹם לַעֲבוֹדָתוֹ· שֶׁנֶּאֱמַר
וַיֹּאמֶר יְהוֹשֻׁעַ אֶל כָּל הָעָם· כֹּה אָמַר יְיָ
אֱלֹהֵי יִשְׂרָאֵל בְּעֵבֶר הַנָּהָר יָשְׁבוּ אֲבוֹתֵיכֶם
מֵעוֹלָם· תֶּרַח אֲבִי אַבְרָהָם וַאֲבִי נָחוֹר·
וַיַּעַבְדוּ אֱלֹהִים אֲחֵרִים: וָאֶקַּח אֶת אֲבִיכֶם
אֶת אַבְרָהָם מֵעֵבֶר הַנָּהָר· וָאוֹלֵךְ אוֹתוֹ
בְּכָל אֶרֶץ כְּנָעַן וָאַרְבֶּה אֶת זַרְעוֹ וָאֶתֶּן לוֹ
אֶת יִצְחָק: וָאֶתֵּן לְיִצְחָק אֶת יַעֲקֹב וְאֶת עֵשָׂו
וָאֶתֵּן לְעֵשָׂו אֶת הַר שֵׂעִיר לָרֶשֶׁת אוֹתוֹ·
וְיַעֲקֹב וּבָנָיו יָרְדוּ מִצְרָיִם:

Australia

South America

India

Southwest Pacific — Aleutian Islands — China

On the Road to Rome - 1944

"Tonight you are eating unleavened bread just as your forebears ate unleavened bread.Because the Exodus came so quickly the dough had no time to rise. There was a time of unleavened bread in this war. The time when it looked as though we might not have time to rise - time to raise an army and equip it, time to stop the onrush of a Germany that was already risen.

" But the bread has begun to rise. It started at Alamein. It was rising higher when the Fifth Army invaded Italy. It is reaching the top of the pan and soon the time will come when it will spread out and into a finished product."

Lt. General Mark W. Clark, commander of the U.S. Fifth Army, addressed Jewish soldiers attending a Seder in Naples, Italy, April 1944.

Why should the telling not begin on the first day of the month of Nissan in which the deliverance took place? Because the verse stresses "on that day," the day on which it began. In that case, should not the telling begin during the day? No, because the text stresses "This commemorates," and you can not say "This" except when the matzah and bitter herbs are set before you.

Originally, our ancestors were idolators, but now the Omnipresent has drawn us to His service, as said (Joshua 24:2-4): "Joshua then said to the entire people: 'This is the word of God, the god of Israel: Long ago your ancestors lived beyond the river (Euphrates) — Terah, Abraham's father and Nahor's father — and they worshipped other gods. But I took your father Abraham from beyond the river and led him through the whole Land of Canaan, and I gave him many descendants: I gave him Isaac, and to Isaac I gave Jacob and Esau. Then I gave Esau the hill country of Seir to possess, while Jacob and his children went down to Egypt."

Sicily — Africa — Persia

בָּרוּךְ שׁוֹמֵר הַבְטָחָתוֹ לְיִשְׂרָאֵל · בָּרוּךְ הוּא · שֶׁהַקָּדוֹשׁ בָּרוּךְ הוּא חִשַּׁב אֶת הַקֵּץ · לַעֲשׂוֹת כְּמָה שֶׁאָמַר לְאַבְרָהָם אָבִינוּ בִּבְרִית בֵּין הַבְּתָרִים · שֶׁנֶּאֱמַר וַיֹּאמֶר לְאַבְרָם יָדֹעַ תֵּדַע כִּי גֵר יִהְיֶה זַרְעֲךָ בְּאֶרֶץ לֹא לָהֶם וַעֲבָדוּם וְעִנּוּ אֹתָם אַרְבַּע מֵאוֹת שָׁנָה: וְגַם אֶת הַגּוֹי אֲשֶׁר יַעֲבֹדוּ דָּן אָנֹכִי וְאַחֲרֵי כֵן יֵצְאוּ בִּרְכֻשׁ גָּדוֹל:

נוטל הכוס בידו ומכסה המצות ואומר :

וְהִיא שֶׁעָמְדָה לַאֲבוֹתֵינוּ וְלָנוּ · שֶׁלֹּא אֶחָד בִּלְבַד עָמַד עָלֵינוּ לְכַלּוֹתֵינוּ · אֶלָּא שֶׁבְּכָל דּוֹר וָדוֹר עוֹמְדִים עָלֵינוּ לְכַלּוֹתֵינוּ · וְהַקָּדוֹשׁ בָּרוּךְ הוּא מַצִּילֵנוּ מִיָּדָם:

מניח הכוס ומגלה המצות כמקדם :

צֵא וּלְמַד · מַה בִּקֵּשׁ לָבָן הָאֲרַמִּי לַעֲשׂוֹת לְיַעֲקֹב אָבִינוּ · שֶׁפַּרְעֹה לֹא גָזַר אֶלָּא עַל הַזְּכָרִים וְלָבָן בִּקֵּשׁ לַעֲקוֹר אֶת הַכֹּל · שֶׁנֶּאֱמַר אֲרַמִּי אֹבֵד אָבִי וַיֵּרֶד מִצְרַיְמָה וַיָּגָר שָׁם בִּמְתֵי מְעָט וַיְהִי שָׁם לְגוֹי גָּדוֹל עָצוּם וָרָב:

U. S. Army Chaplain Abraham Klausner commissioned a special edition Haggadah for U. S. military personnel and displaced persons in 1946. The borders on these two facing pages are impressive woodcuts from the Haggadah which were executed by Y.D. Sheinson. They accompany Chaplain Klausner's English introduction to the Haggadah. The sedarim, where it was used, were held at the Deutsches Theater Restaurant, Munich Germany on April 15-16, 1946 and more than 400 people attended.
In the introduction, Supreme Commander Dwight D. Eisenhower is described as Moses the Liberator and the American forces restore moral order to the world.

Continued on next page.

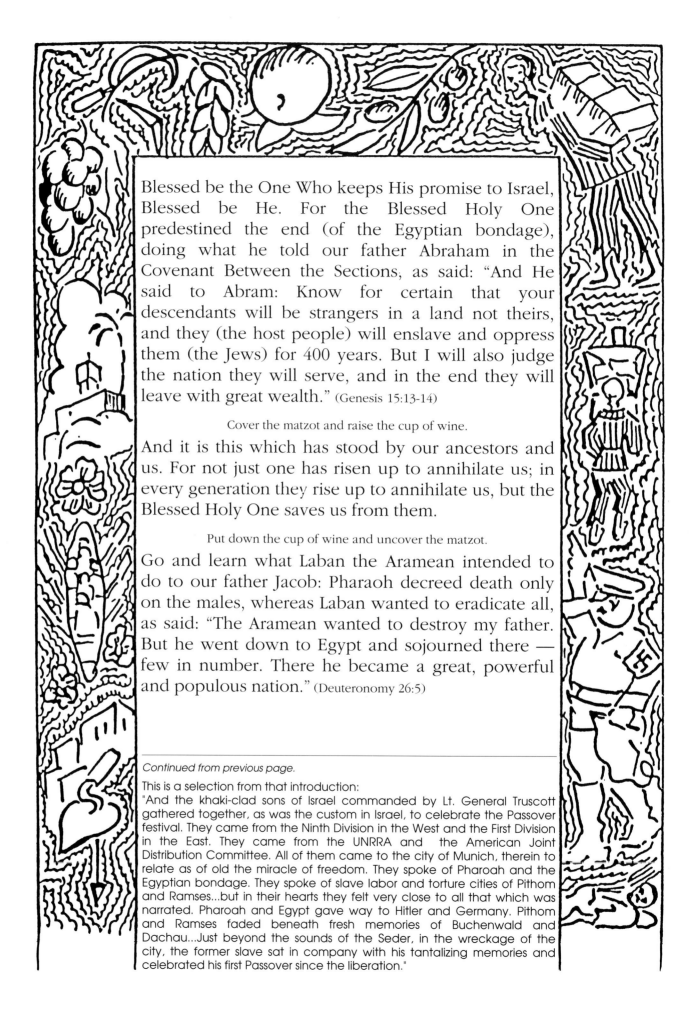

Blessed be the One Who keeps His promise to Israel, Blessed be He. For the Blessed Holy One predestined the end (of the Egyptian bondage), doing what he told our father Abraham in the Covenant Between the Sections, as said: "And He said to Abram: Know for certain that your descendants will be strangers in a land not theirs, and they (the host people) will enslave and oppress them (the Jews) for 400 years. But I will also judge the nation they will serve, and in the end they will leave with great wealth." (Genesis 15:13-14)

Cover the matzot and raise the cup of wine.

And it is this which has stood by our ancestors and us. For not just one has risen up to annihilate us; in every generation they rise up to annihilate us, but the Blessed Holy One saves us from them.

Put down the cup of wine and uncover the matzot.

Go and learn what Laban the Aramean intended to do to our father Jacob: Pharaoh decreed death only on the males, whereas Laban wanted to eradicate all, as said: "The Aramean wanted to destroy my father. But he went down to Egypt and sojourned there — few in number. There he became a great, powerful and populous nation." (Deuteronomy 26:5)

Continued from previous page.

This is a selection from that introduction:
"And the khaki-clad sons of Israel commanded by Lt. General Truscott gathered together, as was the custom in Israel, to celebrate the Passover festival. They came from the Ninth Division in the West and the First Division in the East. They came from the UNRRA and the American Joint Distribution Committee. All of them came to the city of Munich, therein to relate as of old the miracle of freedom. They spoke of Pharoah and the Egyptian bondage. They spoke of slave labor and torture cities of Pithom and Ramses...but in their hearts they felt very close to all that which was narrated. Pharoah and Egypt gave way to Hitler and Germany. Pithom and Ramses faded beneath fresh memories of Buchenwald and Dachau...Just beyond the sounds of the Seder, in the wreckage of the city, the former slave sat in company with his tantalizing memories and celebrated his first Passover since the liberation."

וַיֵּרֶד מִצְרַיְמָה. אָנוּס עַל פִּי הַדִּבּוּר:
וַיָּגָר שָׁם. מְלַמֵּד שֶׁלֹּא יָרַד יַעֲקֹב אָבִינוּ
לְהִשְׁתַּקֵּעַ בְּמִצְרַיִם אֶלָּא לָגוּר שָׁם. שֶׁנֶּאֱמַר
וַיֹּאמְרוּ אֶל פַּרְעֹה לָגוּר בָּאָרֶץ בָּאנוּ כִּי אֵין
מִרְעֶה לַצֹּאן אֲשֶׁר לַעֲבָדֶיךָ כִּי כָבֵד הָרָעָב
בְּאֶרֶץ כְּנָעַן וְעַתָּה יֵשְׁבוּ נָא עֲבָדֶיךָ בְּאֶרֶץ
גֹּשֶׁן: בִּמְתֵי מְעָט. כְּמָה שֶׁנֶּאֱמַר בְּשִׁבְעִים
נֶפֶשׁ יָרְדוּ אֲבֹתֶיךָ מִצְרַיְמָה וְעַתָּה שָׂמְךָ יְיָ
אֱלֹהֶיךָ כְּכוֹכְבֵי הַשָּׁמַיִם לָרֹב: וַיְהִי שָׁם לְגוֹי
גָּדוֹל. מְלַמֵּד שֶׁהָיוּ יִשְׂרָאֵל מְצֻיָּנִים שָׁם:
עָצוּם. כְּמָה שֶׁנֶּאֱמַר וּבְנֵי יִשְׂרָאֵל פָּרוּ וַיִּשְׁרְצוּ
וַיִּרְבּוּ וַיַּעַצְמוּ בִּמְאֹד מְאֹד וַתִּמָּלֵא הָאָרֶץ
אֹתָם: וָרָב. כְּמָה שֶׁנֶּאֱמַר רְבָבָה כְּצֶמַח
הַשָּׂדֶה נְתַתִּיךְ וַתִּרְבִּי וַתִּגְדְּלִי וַתָּבֹאִי
בַּעֲדִי עֲדָיִים שָׁדַיִם נָכֹנוּ וּשְׂעָרֵךְ צִמֵּחַ וְאַתְּ
עֵרֹם וְעֶרְיָה:

וַיָּרֵעוּ אֹתָנוּ הַמִּצְרִים וַיְעַנּוּנוּ וַיִּתְּנוּ עָלֵינוּ
עֲבֹדָה קָשָׁה:

"And the Egyptians made the Children of Israel to serve with rigor."
Ex. 1:13

Barton's Candy Passover Circular 1965. *American Jewish Archives*, Cincinnati, Ohio

וַיָּרֵעוּ אֹתָנוּ הַמִּצְרִים. כְּמָה שֶׁנֶּאֱמַר
הָבָה נִתְחַכְּמָה לוֹ פֶּן יִרְבֶּה וְהָיָה כִּי תִקְרֶאנָה
מִלְחָמָה וְנוֹסַף גַּם הוּא עַל שֹׂנְאֵינוּ וְנִלְחַם
בָּנוּ וְעָלָה מִן הָאָרֶץ: וַיְעַנּוּנוּ. כְּמָה שֶׁנֶּאֱמַר
וַיָּשִׂימוּ עָלָיו שָׂרֵי מִסִּים לְמַעַן עַנֹּתוֹ בְּסִבְלֹתָם
וַיִּבֶן עָרֵי מִסְכְּנוֹת לְפַרְעֹה אֶת פִּתֹם וְאֶת
רַעַמְסֵס: וַיִּתְּנוּ עָלֵינוּ עֲבֹדָה קָשָׁה.
כְּמָה שֶׁנֶּאֱמַר וַיַּעֲבִדוּ מִצְרַיִם אֶת בְּנֵי יִשְׂרָאֵל
בְּפָרֶךְ:

The Living Heritage of Passover
Compiled and edited by Rabbi Solomon S. Bernards, Anti-Defamation League of B'nai B'rith, New York

24

"He went down to Egypt" — compelled to do so by the word of God. "And he sojourned there" — this teaches us that he did not go to settle in Egypt but only to sojourn there, as said: "And they said to Pharaoh: 'We have come to sojourn in the land, as there is no pasture for your servants' sheep, for the famine is severe in the Land of Canaan. Pray, then, let your servants stay in the Goshen region'."

(Genesis 47:4)

"Few in number" — as said: "Just seventy your ancestors numbered when they went down to Egypt; but now God, your god, has made you as numerous as the stars in the sky." (Genesis 47:4)

"There he became a nation" — as said: "But the Children of Israel were fertile and prolific: they increased and became very numerous and the land was full of them." (Exodus 1:7)

"And populous" — as said: "I caused you to increase like wild-flowers, and you throve and grew, and you came to full womanhood, your breasts fully fashioned, your hair grown — but you were still naked and exposed." (Ezekiel 16:7) "Then I came by and saw you writhing helplessly in your own blood, and I said to you: In spite of your blood — live! And I said to you: In spite of your blood — live." (Ezekiel 16:6)

"And the Egyptians ill-treated us and oppressed us, and they imposed hard labor on us." (Deuteronomy 26:6)

"And the Egyptians ill-treated us" — as said: "Let us deal shrewdly with them and prevent them from increasing further, lest — if war breaks out — they join our enemies and fight against us, and take over the country." (Exodus 1:10)

"Oppressed us" — as said: "So they set taskmasters over them in order to oppress them with hard labor. And they built store-cities for Pharaoh: Pithom and Ramses." (Exodus 1:11)

"And they imposed hard labor on us" — as said: "And the Egyptians worked the Children of Israel ruthlessly." (Exodus 1:13)

וַנִּצְעַק אֶל יְיָ אֱלֹהֵי אֲבֹתֵינוּ וַיִּשְׁמַע יְיָ אֶת קֹלֵנוּ וַיַּרְא אֶת עָנְיֵנוּ וְאֶת עֲמָלֵנוּ וְאֶת לַחֲצֵנוּ:

וַנִּצְעַק אֶל יְיָ אֱלֹהֵי אֲבֹתֵינוּ · כְּמָה שֶׁנֶּאֱמַר וַיְהִי בַיָּמִים הָרַבִּים הָהֵם וַיָּמָת מֶלֶךְ מִצְרַיִם וַיֵּאָנְחוּ בְנֵי יִשְׂרָאֵל · מִן הָעֲבֹדָה: וַיִּזְעָקוּ וַתַּעַל שַׁוְעָתָם אֶל הָאֱלֹהִים מִן הָעֲבֹדָה: וַיִּשְׁמַע יְיָ אֶת קֹלֵנוּ · כְּמָה שֶׁנֶּאֱמַר וַיִּשְׁמַע אֱלֹהִים אֶת נַאֲקָתָם וַיִּזְכֹּר אֱלֹהִים אֶת בְּרִיתוֹ אֶת אַבְרָהָם אֶת יִצְחָק וְאֶת יַעֲקֹב: וַיַּרְא אֶת עָנְיֵנוּ · זוֹ פְּרִישׁוּת דֶּרֶךְ אֶרֶץ · כְּמָה שֶׁנֶּאֱמַר וַיַּרְא אֱלֹהִים אֶת בְּנֵי יִשְׂרָאֵל וַיֵּדַע אֱלֹהִים: וְאֶת עֲמָלֵנוּ · אֵלּוּ הַבָּנִים · כְּמָה שֶׁנֶּאֱמַר כָּל הַבֵּן הַיִּלּוֹד הַיְאֹרָה תַּשְׁלִיכֻהוּ וְכָל הַבַּת תְּחַיּוּן: וְאֶת לַחֲצֵנוּ · זֶה הַדַּחַק · כְּמָה שֶׁנֶּאֱמַר וְגַם רָאִיתִי אֶת הַלַּחַץ אֲשֶׁר מִצְרַיִם לֹחֲצִים אֹתָם:

Moses Smiting the Egyptian

The artist for the Liberman-Chicago Haggadah utilized earlier European depictions of Moses killing the Egyptian taskmaster. However, this American drawing differs from those versions in that Pithom and Ramses, the Egyptian cities under construction, contain only buildings with flat roofs and columns. Furthermore, in America in the 1870s, pulleys were used to construct buildings and are shown here. The artist may have been influenced by the builders whom he saw in Chicago.

Haggadah for Passover ed. Hayyim Liberman, Chicago, 1879

"Then we cried out to God, the god of our fathers, and God heard our voice and He saw our ill-treatment, our hardship and our distress."

(Deuteronomy 26:7)

"Then we cried out to God, the god of our fathers" — as said: "Long after that, the King of Egypt died. But the Children of Israel were still in grinding slavery, and they cried out, and their outcry about their slavery reached God." (Exodus 2:23)

"God heard our voice" — as said: "And God heard their groaning, and God remembered His covenant with Abraham, with Isaac and with Jacob." (Exodus 2:24)

"And He saw our ill-treatment" — this was a forced separation of husbands from their wives, as said: "And God saw the Children of Israel, and God knew." (Exodus 2:25)

"Our hardship" — this means the sons, as said: "Every newborn boy you shall throw into the Nile, but let every girl live." (Exodus 1:22)

"And our distress" — this refers to the brutality, as said: "I have also seen the brutality with which the Egyptians are oppressing them." (Exodus 3:9)

A Long Arm Saves Baby Moses from the Nile
Many Talmudic legends relate to the discovery of Moses as described in the Bible. This Liberman-Chicago Haggadah drawing is influenced by these legends. As Moses floats in his reed basket, the daughter of Pharoah with her entourage come to the water's edge to bathe. As the illustration emphasizes, other Jewish children are drowning, but a protected Moses floats safely, waiting to be saved. Unfortunately, his basket is not close enough to shore and, according to rabbinic legend, God lengthens the arm of a handmaiden of Pharoah's daughter and thus Moses is rescued.

Haggadah for Passover
ed. Hayyim Liberman, Chicago, 1879

27

וַיּוֹצִ**אֵ**נוּ יְיָ מִמִּצְרַיִם בְּיָד חֲזָקָה וּבִזְרֹעַ
נְטוּיָה וּבְמֹרָא גָּדֹל וּבְאוֹתֹת וּבְמֹפְתִים:
וַיּוֹצִיאֵנוּ יְיָ מִמִּצְרַיִם. לֹא עַל יְדֵי מַלְאָךְ.
וְלֹא עַל יְדֵי שָׂרָף. וְלֹא עַל יְדֵי שָׁלִיחַ. אֶלָּא
הַקָּדוֹשׁ בָּרוּךְ הוּא בִּכְבוֹדוֹ וּבְעַצְמוֹ שֶׁנֶּ**אֱ**מַר
וְעָבַרְתִּי בְאֶרֶץ־מִצְרַיִם בַּלַּיְלָה הַזֶּה וְהִכֵּיתִי
כָל־בְּכוֹר בְּאֶרֶץ מִצְרַיִם מֵאָדָם וְעַד־בְּהֵמָה
וּבְכָל־אֱלֹהֵי מִצְרַיִם אֶעֱשֶׂה שְׁפָטִים אֲנִי יְיָ:

וְעָבַרְתִּי בְאֶרֶץ מִצְרַיִם. אֲנִי וְלֹא מַלְאָךְ.
וְהִכֵּיתִי כָל בְּכוֹר. אֲנִי וְלֹא שָׂרָף. וּבְכָל אֱלֹהֵי
מִצְרַיִם אֶעֱשֶׂה שְׁפָטִים. אֲנִי וְלֹא הַשָּׁלִיחַ. אֲנִי יְיָ.
אֲנִי הוּא וְלֹא אַחֵר:

בְּיָד חֲזָקָה זוֹ הַדֶּבֶר. כְּמָה שֶׁנֶּ**אֱ**מַר
הִנֵּה יַד־יְיָ הוֹיָה בְּמִקְנְךָ אֲשֶׁר בַּשָּׂדֶה בַּסּוּסִים
בַּחֲמֹרִים בַּגְּמַלִּים בַּבָּקָר וּבַצֹּאן דֶּבֶר כָּבֵד
מְא**ֹ**ד: וּבִזְרֹעַ נְטוּיָה. זוֹ הַחֶרֶב. כְּמָה
שֶׁנֶּ**אֱ**מַר וְחַרְבּוֹ שְׁלוּפָה בְּיָדוֹ נְטוּיָה עַל־
יְרוּשָׁלָ͏ִם. וּבְמֹרָא גָּדֹל זוֹ גִּלּוּי שְׁכִינָה.
כְּמָה שֶׁנֶּאֱמַר אוֹ הֲנִסָּה אֱלֹהִים לָבוֹא לָקַחַת
לוֹ גוֹי מִקֶּרֶב גּוֹי בְּמַסֹּת בְּאֹתֹת וּבְמוֹפְתִים
וּבְמִלְחָמָה וּבְיָד חֲזָקָה וּבִזְרוֹעַ נְטוּיָה וּבְמוֹרָאִים
גְּדֹלִים כְּכֹל אֲשֶׁר־עָשָׂה לָכֶם יְיָ אֱלֹהֵיכֶם
בְּמִצְרַיִם לְעֵינֶיךָ: וּבְאֹתוֹת. זֶה הַמַּטֶּה.
כְּמָה שֶׁנֶּאֱמַר וְאֶת־הַמַּטֶּה הַזֶּה תִּקַּח בְּיָדְךָ

PERSONAL MEMORIES OF PASSOVER ON THE EAST SIDE
by Sidney Roth

On the lower East Side, 40 or 50 years ago, Passover preparations started months before the holiday. Beginning about Chanukah, when my mother went shopping for chickens, for "Shabbos," she bought only chickens with a lot of fat, because now was the time to start saving "Schmaltz for Pesach."

And who could have too much "Schmaltz for Pesach?" You needed it for the "Chremslach," for the potato "latkes," for "Matzo-Brei" and even just to put on a slice of Matzo with a little bit of salt. You needed "Schmaltz" because Pesach was a "Fleishashig Yomtov." Don't forget this was in the days before "Nyafat" and the Rokeach family was only making kosher soap for washing dishes. There were no "Heshgochos" for canned foods, chocolate candy was "Avada" "chomitz." So there was very little you could have with matzo except the schmaltz.

So mama started collecting chicken fat which she kept in a special stone "Pesachdige" crock, covered with a blanket, in a corner that was already prepared for Pesach.

Next, after Purim, it was time to start making "Russel," and sure enough, on Rivington Street, you'd see pushcarts with "Lange Burkis," just the kind of beets that were needed to begin preparing what would be Borsht for the holiday.

Now it was also time to talk about buying new clothes for the Yomtov. Everybody had to get something new. Even if there wasn't enough money to buy all new clothes, at least new shoes for everybody was a must. Finally it was 2 days before Erev Yomtov and it was time to get the Pesachdigge dishes ready.

Now let me explain a bit. In the cellar, in every tenement, there were little locked cubbyholes for each family, where they kept the things there was no room for in the apartment upstairs. With all the children, and even a boarder, now and then and hardly any closets, there was hardly any room for people upstairs. In the cellar, then, were stored the pesachdigge dishes, pots, glasses and silverware, wrapped in newspaper and left there from one year to the next. The pots had to be brought up right away and cleaned so that the cooking could start for the Yomtov. Then each of the dishes,

Continued on next page.

Continued from previous page.

glasses and silverware had to be unpacked and washed and believe me, with all the milichiga dishes and enough fleishidig dishes to feed at least 50 people at the Seder, two days wasn't too much time to get the dishes ready.

Finally, it was the evening of Erev Pesach and as the oldest son, it was my job to go around with my father to collect the pieces of "Chometz" which he had put around the house. I held a lighted candle while my father brushed the pieces of bread with a chicken feather into the wooden spoon he was holding in a piece of rag. After he counted to make sure that all the pieces of bread had been collected, he blew out the candle, put it in the spoon with the pieces of bread and the feather and tied it all together in the rag. Then he gave the bundle to me. Next morning, I took it downstairs, lit a fire and burned it.

All over the East Side, as the morning wore on, you could feel the holiday coming nearer and nearer. The smell of holiday food cooking, the sight of men coming home from work, many hours before they would have ordinarily, to get ready for the celebration, and as it became later and later, seeing the stores closing, one after the other, you knew that Yomtov was here and on this night, in this neighborhood, only the drugstore on the corner would stay open; everybody else would celebrate.

Of course, all the men went to Shul, were freshly bathed and dressed in their finest, they took part in the Ma'ariv service while the mothers of the families were trying to get finished with the last minute preparations, getting dressed and taking care of the little children, all at the same time.

After all these preparations, the moment had arrived. Seats were found for everyone and with eleven children, a few uncles and aunts, several cousins, landsleit and even a yeshiva bucher or two, who were away from home, there were at least 50 people at the Seder table. And then the Seder began.

American Jewish Archives
Cincinnati, Ohio

"And God brought us out of Egypt with a strong hand and an outstretched arm and with terrifying deeds, and with signs and with portents."

(Deuteronomy 26:8)

"And God brought us out of Egypt" — not through an angel, and not through a seraph, and not through a messenger, but the Blessed Holy One Himself, as said: "On that night I will pass through the land of Egypt and I will kill every firstborn in the land of Egypt, human and beast; on all the gods of Egypt I will execute judgement — I, God." (Exodus 12:12)

"On that night I will pass through the land of Egypt" — I, not an angel. "And I will kill every firstborn in the land of Egypt" — I, not a seraph. "On all the gods of Egypt I will execute judgement" — I, not a messenger. I, God — I am the one; nobody else.

"With a strong hand" — this is the pestilence, as said: "Then God's hand will strike your grazing herds — the horses, the asses, the camels, the cattle and the sheep — with a very severe pestilence." (Exodus 9:3)

"And an outstretched arm" — this is the sword, as said: "...with his sword drawn in his hand outstretched over Jerusalem." (I Chronicles 21:16)

"And with terrifying deeds" — this is the appearance of the Divine Presence, as said: "Has a god ever ventured to come and take himself a nation from within another nation by miracles, by signs and portents, and by war, by a mighty hand and an outstretched arm and by great deeds of terror as God, your god, did for you in Egypt before your very very eyes?" (Deuteronomy 4:34)

"By signs" — this is the rod, as said: "And take along

אֲשֶׁר תַּעֲשֶׂה־בּוֹ אֶת־הָאֹתֹת: וּבְמֹפְתִים
זֶה הַדָּם. כְּמָה שֶׁנֶּאֱמַר וְנָתַתִּי מוֹפְתִים
בַּשָּׁמַיִם וּבָאָרֶץ. דָּם. וָאֵשׁ. וְתִימְרוֹת
עָשָׁן. דָּבָר אַחֵר. בְּיָד חֲזָקָה שְׁתַּיִם. וּבִזְרֹעַ
נְטוּיָה שְׁתַּיִם. וּבְמֹרָא גָּדֹל שְׁתַּיִם. וּבְאֹתוֹת
שְׁתַּיִם. וּבְמֹפְתִים שְׁתַּיִם: אֵלּוּ עֶשֶׂר מַכּוֹת
שֶׁהֵבִיא הַקָּדוֹשׁ בָּרוּךְ הוּא עַל הַמִּצְרִים
בְּמִצְרַיִם: וְאֵלּוּ הֵן:

דָּם. צְפַרְדֵּעַ. כִּנִּים. עָרוֹב
דֶּבֶר. שְׁחִין. בָּרָד. אַרְבֶּה
חֹשֶׁךְ. מַכַּת בְּכוֹרוֹת:

רַבִּי יְהוּדָה הָיָה נוֹתֵן בָּהֶם סִמָּנִים.
דְּצַ"ךְ עֲדַ"שׁ בְּאַחַ"ב:

The ten plagues are remembered by dipping the finger ten times into the wine and naming a plague at each dipping. This seder was held at the Home of the Sons and Daughters of Israel in New York, April 1938.
LIFE, April 18, 1938

The Ten Plagues
The illustrations of the ten plagues on these two pages originated in Europe. They appear in the Hebrew-English version of the Haggadah published in New York in 1857 by L. H. Frank.

this rod with which you shall perform the signs."

(Exodus 4:17)

"And with portents" — this is the blood, as said: "I will show portents in the sky and on earth:

blood
fire and
pillars of smoke"

(Joel 3:3)

Another explanation: "By a mighty hand" — two; "and an outstretched arm" — two; "and by great deeds of terror" — two; "by signs" — two; "and portents" — two.

These are ten plagues which the Blessed Holy One brought on the Egyptians in Egypt:

Blood • *Frogs* • *Lice*
Wild beasts • *Murrain* • *Boils*
Hail • *Locust* • *Darkness*
• *The smiting of the firstborn* •

Rabbi Yehuda made a mnemonic of them:

DeTZaKh ADaSH BeAHaB

THE JEWS
Again the Wandering Children of Israel are on the Move in Hostile Europe
Now at Passover they celebrate their Exodus from Egypt.

On the broad stream of history, Franklin D. Roosevelt has just tossed a straw. The ripples it made spread into the foreign ministries of two hemispheres, most of which rippled back earnest approval. Then all ripples died away.

What the president had done was remind the world that it was beset with an acute refugee problem. In all lands, he said, were unwanted minorities - millions of people for whom haven should be found. The president specified refugees in Russia, Italy, Spain. But the world well understood that he really meant the greatest of all refugees, the Jews who are the world's eternal wanderers and who once again must take up their unresting march from countries which once welcomed them and no longer will tolerate them. They are besieged in Germany and Austria, persecuted in Poland, oppressed in Rumania.

At this time, on the first night of Passover, which falls on April 15, the Jew throughout the world gathers his family about his table for the Seder ceremony to tell of the greatest of all his wanderings - the Exodus from Egypt. At the Seder, the head of the family says: "This year we are here, next year we shall be in the land of Israel."

This hope, echoing down the generations of Jewry, has an especial irony now when the Jew, instead of returning to a homeland, must disperse over the world in the search of safety and the simple grace of peace. But the Seder, symbolizing his deliverance from bondage in Egypt, is a happy occasion.

LIFE, April 18, 1938

רַבִּי יוֹסֵי הַגְּלִילִי אוֹמֵר· מִנַּיִן אַתָּה אוֹמֵר
שֶׁלָּקוּ הַמִּצְרִיִּים בְּמִצְרַיִם עֶשֶׂר מַכּוֹת· וְעַל
הַיָּם לָקוּ חֲמִשִּׁים מַכּוֹת· בְּמִצְרַיִם מַה הוּא
אוֹמֵר וַיֹּאמְרוּ הַחַרְטֻמִּם אֶל־פַּרְעֹה אֶצְבַּע
אֱלֹהִים הוּא: וְעַל הַיָּם מַה הוּא אוֹמֵר וַיַּרְא
יִשְׂרָאֵל אֶת־הַיָּד הַגְּדֹלָה אֲשֶׁר עָשָׂה יְיָ בְּמִצְרַיִם
וַיִּירְאוּ הָעָם אֶת־יְיָ וַיַּאֲמִינוּ בַּיְיָ וּבְמֹשֶׁה עַבְדּוֹ:
כַּמָּה לָקוּ בְאֶצְבַּע· עֶשֶׂר מַכּוֹת· אֱמוֹר
מֵעַתָּה בְּמִצְרַיִם לָקוּ עֶשֶׂר מַכּוֹת· וְעַל הַיָּם
לָקוּ חֲמִשִּׁים מַכּוֹת:

רַבִּי אֱלִיעֶזֶר אוֹמֵר· מִנַּיִן שֶׁכָּל מַכָּה וּמַכָּה
שֶׁהֵבִיא הַקָּדוֹשׁ בָּרוּךְ הוּא עַל הַמִּצְרִיִּים
בְּמִצְרַיִם הָיְתָה שֶׁל אַרְבַּע מַכּוֹת· שֶׁנֶּאֱמַר
יְשַׁלַּח־בָּם חֲרוֹן אַפּוֹ עֶבְרָה וָזַעַם וְצָרָה
מִשְׁלַחַת מַלְאֲכֵי רָעִים: עֶבְרָה אַחַת· וָזַעַם
שְׁתַּיִם· וְצָרָה שָׁלֹשׁ· מִשְׁלַחַת מַלְאֲכֵי רָעִים
אַרְבַּע· אֱמוֹר מֵעַתָּה בְּמִצְרַיִם לָקוּ אַרְבָּעִים
מַכּוֹת· וְעַל הַיָּם לָקוּ מָאתַיִם מַכּוֹת:

רַבִּי עֲקִיבָא אוֹמֵר· מִנַּיִן שֶׁכָּל מַכָּה וּמַכָּה
שֶׁהֵבִיא הַקָּדוֹשׁ בָּרוּךְ הוּא עַל הַמִּצְרִיִּים
בְּמִצְרַיִם הָיְתָה שֶׁל חָמֵשׁ מַכּוֹת· שֶׁנֶּאֱמַר
יְשַׁלַּח־בָּם חֲרוֹן אַפּוֹ עֶבְרָה וָזַעַם וְצָרָה מִשְׁלַחַת
מַלְאֲכֵי רָעִים· חֲרוֹן אַפּוֹ אַחַת· עֶבְרָה שְׁתַּיִם·
וָזַעַם שָׁלֹשׁ· וְצָרָה אַרְבַּע· מִשְׁלַחַת מַלְאֲכֵי
רָעִים חָמֵשׁ· אֱמוֹר מֵעַתָּה בְּמִצְרַיִם לָקוּ
חֲמִשִּׁים מַכּוֹת· וְעַל הַיָּם לָקוּ חֲמִשִּׁים
וּמָאתַיִם מַכּוֹת:

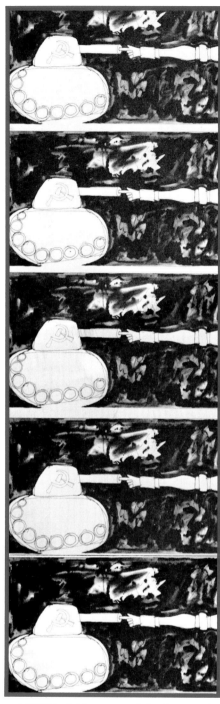

The fivefold power of the finger of
God is depicted by Mark Podwal
halting the Russian tanks. When he
drew these illustrations, he did not
realize that he might be prophetic. The
following year in 1973, when the Yom
Kippur War broke out, the Russian
tanks used by the Syrians and
Egyptians were halted not only by
Israeli tank commanders but also
perhaps by the finger of God.

Let My People Go: A Haggadah by
Mark Podwal, New York, 1972
Used by permission of
Dr. Mark Podwal

32

At the Seashore of Eternity

The Passover is Israel's watchnight, Israel's redoubt from which the presence of God in the world and in history is discernible, ready to bring succor even though overwhelming forces of facts beat upon it to destroy. For at Passover, Israel with God saw the Egyptians destroyed at the seashore, an experience which repeated itself in the course of the centuries. Babylon, the great, passed, leaving only records of former grandeur and conquest. Ancient Persia is no more. Greece and Rome whose pride and dominion humbled Israel and broke its national power are like Egyptian wreckage on the seashore of eternity.

Since the mighty deliverance wrought in Egypt till today, Israel with God has ploughed through the fields of time, sowing in its furrows the seed of religious experience and of religious health. Year after year the sons of Jacob, gathered in their homes for the seder on Passover eve, were fortified in the belief of their fathers and in the assurance of God's promise to their children. Their existence is living testimony; they are eye witnesses. For here is a people, weak, scattered, without land, which survives inhuman persecution, here is a people who outlives its vanquishers, here is a conquered who triumphs over the conquerer.

"American Israel's Opportunity" Passover Sermon by Rev. Dr. Nathan Stern at the West End Synagogue in New York, April 7, 1917. American Jewish Archives, Cincinnati Ohio

Rabbi Yossé the Galilean says: How do you reckon that the Egyptians were smitten with ten plagues in Egypt and with fifty plagues on the sea? Concerning Egypt what does it say? "And the wizards said to Pharaoh: 'This is the finger of God'!" (Exodus 8:15) And concerning the sea what does it say? "And Israel saw the wondrous hand that God had wielded against the Egyptians, and the people feared God, and they put their trust in God and in His servant Moses." (Exodus 14:31) With how many plagues were they smitten with a finger? Ten plagues. Hence, in Egypt they were smitten with ten plagues, and on the sea they were smitten with fifty plagues.

Rabbi Eliezer says: How do we know that each plague that the Blessed Holy One brought on the Egyptians in Egypt consisted of four plagues? For it is said: "He loosed upon them His burning anger: wrath, and fury, and rage a legation of evil messengers." (Psalms 78:49)
"Wrath" — one. "And fury" — one. "And rage" — one. "A legation of evil messengers" — one.
Hence, in Egypt they were smitten with forty plagues, and on the sea they were smitten with 200 plagues.

Rabbi Akiva says: How do we know that each plague that the Blessed Holy One brought on the Egyptians in Egypt consisted of five plagues? For it is said: "He loosed upon them His burning anger, wrath, and fury, and rage, a legation of evil messengers." (Psalms 78:49)
"His burning anger" — one. "Wrath" — two. "And fury" — three. "And rage" — four. "A legation of evil messengers" — five.
Hence, in Egypt they were smitten with fifty plagues, and on the sea they were smitten with 250 plagues.

כַּמָה מַעֲלוֹת טוֹבוֹת לַמָקוֹם עָלֵינוּ:

אִלוּ הוֹצִיאָנוּ מִמִצְרַיִם· וְלֹא עָשָׂה
בָהֶם שְׁפָטִים דַיֵנוּ:

אִלוּ עָשָׂה בָהֶם שְׁפָטִים· וְלֹא עָשָׂה
בֵאלֹהֵיהֶם דַיֵנוּ:

אִלוּ עָשָׂה בֵאלֹהֵיהֶם· וְלֹא הָרַג
בְּכוֹרֵיהֶם דַיֵנוּ:

אִלוּ הָרַג בְּכוֹרֵיהֶם· וְלֹא נָתַן לָנוּ אֶת
מָמוֹנָם דַיֵנוּ:

אִלוּ נָתַן לָנוּ אֶת מָמוֹנָם· וְלֹא קָרַע לָנוּ
אֶת הַיָּם דַיֵנוּ:

אִלוּ קָרַע לָנוּ אֶת הַיָּם· וְלֹא הֶעֱבִירָנוּ
בְּתוֹכוֹ בֶּחָרָבָה דַיֵנוּ:

אִלוּ הֶעֱבִירָנוּ בְּתוֹכוֹ בֶּחָרָבָה· וְלֹא שִׁקַע
צָרֵינוּ בְּתוֹכוֹ דַיֵנוּ:

**On the Other Side
of the Curtain**
by Zalman Shazar

Leavened food is on my table,
Nothing festive in my room.
No one heeds me celebrating
My seder in this gloom.
I celebrate my seder
Soundlessly, alone -
Now my room is fit for Pesach
And I feast on bitter herbs.
Reading with my lips closed tight
The Haggadah's ancient rite,
I raise my silence higher,
Higher than the highest tone,
Reading "Slaves were we."
Filled with poison to the brink
Is the glass I lift and drink.
I remember and I ponder
On the Warsaw that once was,
While in a dream there comes
A letter sent from Tel Aviv.
Pondering I wonder
How different this chapter,
And in my dream I note
Water, sail and boat.
Then my room grows brighter
And my table more Kasher
I sing out at my seder
While no one pays me heed.
I sing out all the higher
At "Dayenu" and "L'chaim."
I lift my glass in silence
"Next year in Yerushalayim!"

Zalman Shazar, the third president of
the State of Israel, gave this poem at a
Third Seder of the Histadrut held in
New York in 1956.
Originating in the USA, the Third Seder
was a way of raising funds for
organizations such as the Workmen's
Circle, Histadrut, Labor Zionists,
Revisionists, Mizrachi. This poem was
translated from the Yiddish by Mrs.
Shulamit Nardi, Adviser to the
presidents of Israel since 1958.

That Would Have Been *Good Enough*

Red Sea - Atlantic Ocean

Then did God Himself provide them with a Moses who led them through the Red Sea. You, my friends, were also treated as slaves in dark Russia and were also led through the Red Sea, but it was red from the blood which the Russian barbarians have shed of many innocent men, women and children, red from the flames which issued from your burnt houses. Instead of being rewarded as your ancestors were, who left Egypt, you were even robbed of all your worldly possessions; from behind you were pursued by the Czar with his officers, and in front of you were confronted by the Atlantic Ocean. But instead of a single Moses in Egypt, there were several such found in America, who have not only emancipated you, but are endeavoring to provide for your future.

Address at Ward's Island, New York, Seder for immigrants, April 1882

Jews Not Compelled to Mark Own Ballots at Election on Passover

Chicago, April 1 - Orthodox Jews who were threatened with the loss of their votes in the Mayoralty contest because Election Day, April 6, is the last day of Passover, are rejoicing because the Election Board has found a means of aiding them. A resolution has been passed instructing judges and clerks of election to mark ballots for Orthodox Jews, who are prohibited from manual labor of any description even to marking ballots on this holiday.

The resolution carries out a ruling by County Judge Sculley that a clerk and judge of election of opposite political faith shall enter the booth with any man or woman affected by the order and mark the ballot according to voter's direction.

Chicago Sun-Times April 2, 1915

So many are the favors for which we must thank the Omnipresent One!

If He had taken us out of Egypt but not given them their punishments —

That would have been good enough!

If He had given them their punishments but not taken it out on their gods —

That would have been good enough!

If He had taken it out on their gods but not killed their firstborn —

That would have been good enough!

If He had killed their firstborn but not handed us their wealth —

That would have been good enough!

If He had handed us their wealth but not parted the sea for us —

That would have been good enough!

If He had parted the sea for us but not brought us through it dry —

That would have been good enough!

If He had brought us through it dry but not sunk our enemies in it —

That would have been good enough!

אִלּוּ שִׁקַּע צָרֵינוּ בְּתוֹכוֹ· וְלֹא סִפֵּק צָרְכֵנוּ
בַּמִּדְבָּר אַרְבָּעִים שָׁנָה דַּיֵּנוּ:

אִלּוּ סִפֵּק צָרְכֵנוּ בַּמִּדְבָּר אַרְבָּעִים שָׁנָה·
וְלֹא הֶאֱכִילָנוּ אֶת הַמָּן דַּיֵּנוּ:

אִלּוּ הֶאֱכִילָנוּ אֶת הַמָּן· וְלֹא נָתַן לָנוּ אֶת
הַשַּׁבָּת דַּיֵּנוּ:

אִלּוּ נָתַן לָנוּ אֶת הַשַּׁבָּת· וְלֹא קֵרְבָנוּ לִפְנֵי
הַר סִינַי דַּיֵּנוּ:

אִלּוּ קֵרְבָנוּ לִפְנֵי הַר סִינַי· וְלֹא נָתַן לָנוּ
אֶת הַתּוֹרָה דַּיֵּנוּ:

אִלּוּ נָתַן לָנוּ אֶת הַתּוֹרָה· וְלֹא הִכְנִיסָנוּ
לְאֶרֶץ יִשְׂרָאֵל דַּיֵּנוּ:

אִלּוּ הִכְנִיסָנוּ לְאֶרֶץ יִשְׂרָאֵל· וְלֹא בָנָה לָנוּ
אֶת בֵּית הַבְּחִירָה דַּיֵּנוּ:

HEBREW CLASS
OF
TEMPLE BNAI ISRAEL
APRIL 3, 1938.

If He had sunk our enemies in it but not provided for us in the wilderness for forty years —
That would have been good enough!

If He had provided for us in the wilderness for forty years but not fed us the manna —
That would have been good enough!

If He had fed us the manna but not given us the Sabbath —
That would have been good enough!

If He had given us the Sabbath but not drawn us near to Him at Mount Sinai —
That would have been good enough!

If He had drawn us near to Him at Mount Sinai but not given us the Torah —
That would have been good enough!

If He had given us the Torah but not brought us into the Land of Israel —
That would have been good enough!

If He had brought us into the Land of Israel but not built us the House of His Choosing —
That would have been good enough!

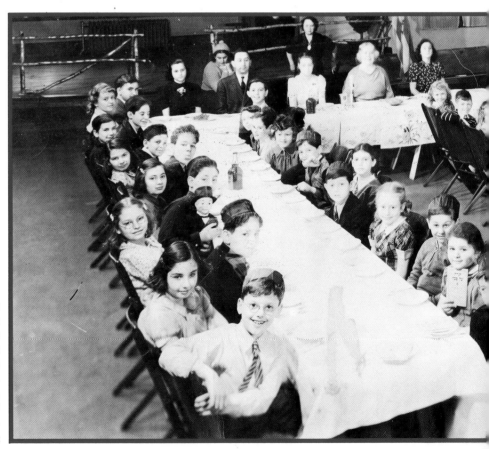

The model seder for children has become an annual event held before Passover each year. At this seder in 1938 one unexpected guest is the puppet, Charley McCarthy, held by a boy on the left side of the picture. Another participant reacts with his tongue to the photographer. This photograph was discovered in Jerusalem, and the synagogue locale of the seder is either in the state of Ohio or Connecticut.

Rafi Grafman Collection

עַל אַחַת כַּמָּה וְכַמָּה טוֹבָה כְפוּלָה וּמְכֻפֶּלֶת
לַמָּקוֹם עָלֵינוּ· שֶׁהוֹצִיאָנוּ מִמִּצְרַיִם· וְעָשָׂה
בָהֶם שְׁפָטִים· וְעָשָׂה בֵאלֹהֵיהֶם· וְהָרַג בְּכוֹרֵיהֶם·
וְנָתַן לָנוּ אֶת מָמוֹנָם· וְקָרַע לָנוּ אֶת הַיָּם·
וְהֶעֱבִירָנוּ בְתוֹכוֹ בֶּחָרָבָה· וְשִׁקַּע צָרֵינוּ בְּתוֹכוֹ·
וְסִפֵּק צָרְכֵּנוּ בַּמִּדְבָּר אַרְבָּעִים שָׁנָה·
וְהֶאֱכִילָנוּ אֶת הַמָּן· וְנָתַן לָנוּ אֶת הַשַּׁבָּת·
וְקֵרְבָנוּ לִפְנֵי הַר סִינַי· וְנָתַן לָנוּ אֶת הַתּוֹרָה·
וְהִכְנִיסָנוּ לְאֶרֶץ יִשְׂרָאֵל· וּבָנָה לָנוּ אֶת בֵּית
הַבְּחִירָה לְכַפֵּר עַל כָּל עֲוֹנוֹתֵינוּ:

רַבָּן גַּמְלִיאֵל הָיָה אוֹמֵר· כָּל שֶׁלֹּא אָמַר
שְׁלֹשָׁה דְבָרִים אֵלּוּ בַּפֶּסַח לֹא יָצָא יְדֵי
חוֹבָתוֹ וְאֵלּוּ הֵן·

פֶּסַח מַצָּה וּמָרוֹר·

פֶּסַח שֶׁהָיוּ אֲבוֹתֵינוּ אוֹכְלִים בִּזְמַן שֶׁבֵּית
הַמִּקְדָּשׁ קַיָּם· עַל שׁוּם מָה· עַל שׁוּם שֶׁפָּסַח
הַקָּדוֹשׁ בָּרוּךְ הוּא עַל בָּתֵּי אֲבוֹתֵינוּ בְּמִצְרַיִם·
שֶׁנֶּאֱמַר וַאֲמַרְתֶּם זֶבַח פֶּסַח הוּא לַיְיָ אֲשֶׁר
פָּסַח עַל־בָּתֵּי בְנֵי־יִשְׂרָאֵל בְּמִצְרַיִם בְּנָגְפּוֹ אֶת־
מִצְרַיִם וְאֶת־בָּתֵּינוּ הִצִּיל וַיִּקֹּד הָעָם וַיִּשְׁתַּחֲווּ:

The Seal of Freedom

Freedom is the great message of Passover summed up in God's words to Pharoah: "let My people go!" This is a fundamental Jewish ideal, expressed in the opening words of the Ten Commandments: "I am the Lord your God who brought you out of the land of Egypt, out of the house of bondage."

Though the exodus of Israel from Egypt took place more than 3000 years ago, no event in our history is impressed more deeply on Jewish minds than the story told in the Haggadah and reenacted each year for the past hundred generations. Through the centuries this story has inspired men and nations to work and pray and, if need be, to fight for freedom.

The spark which fired the soul of America in colonial days and led to the Declaration of Independence was struck from the pulpits and pamphlets of religious and secular preachers who recalled to the Bible-reading colonists the success of Israel's ancient struggle for liberty.

The Declaration itself religiously reminds the world "that all men are created equal, that they are endowed by their Creator with certain inalienable rights, that among these are Life, Liberty and the pursuit of Happiness."

On the day the Declaration of Independence was signed, July 4, 1776, Benjamin Franklin, Thomas Jefferson and John Adams were chosen to design a seal for the new nation. The seal they submitted portrayed the victorious Moses and the defeated Pharoah at the Red Sea. The motto around the picture reads: "Rebellion to tyrants is obedience to God."

Passover Seder Guide
ed. Chaplain Norman Patz
Camp Lejeune, North Carolina April 1967.

How many times more, then, do we owe thanks to the Omnipresent for taking us out of Egypt, and giving them their just deserts, and taking it out on their gods, and killing their firstborn, and handing us their wealth, and splitting the sea for us, and bringing us through it dry, and sinking our oppressors in it, and providing for us in the wilderness for forty years, and feeding us manna, and giving us the Sabbath, and drawing us near to Him at Mount Sinai, and giving us the Torah, and bringing us into Eretz Yisrael, and building us the House of His Choosing for the expiation of all our sins.

Rabbi Gamliel used to say: Whoever has not mentioned these three things on Passover has not fulfilled his obligation:

The Passover Offering
Matzah
Bitter Herbs

The Passover Offering which our ancestors ate when the Temple was standing — what was the reason for it? Because the Blessed Holy One passed over our ancestors' houses in Egypt, as said: "You shall say: It is a Passover sacrifice to God, because He passed over the houses of the Children of Israel in Egypt when He smote the Egyptians but spared our houses. And the people bowed down and prostrated themselves." (Exodus 12:27)

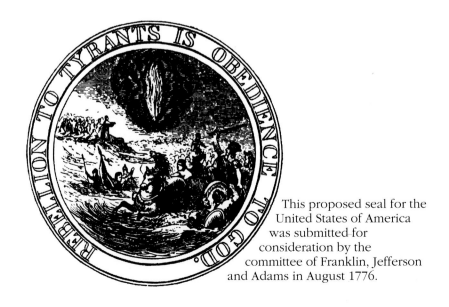

This proposed seal for the United States of America was submitted for consideration by the committee of Franklin, Jefferson and Adams in August 1776.

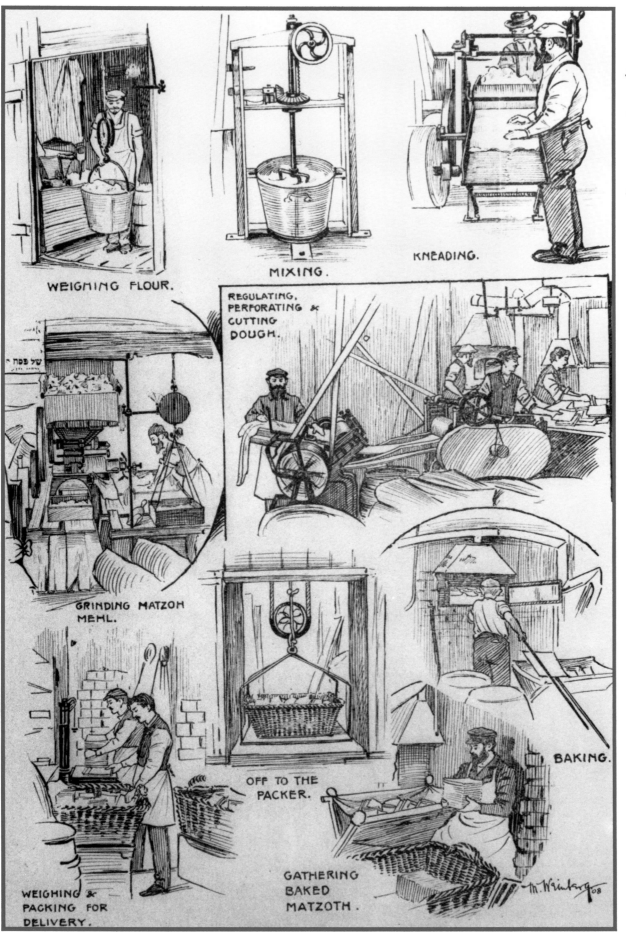

WEIGHING FLOUR.

MIXING.

KNEADING.

REGULATING, PERFORATING & CUTTING DOUGH.

GRINDING MATZOH MEHL.

OFF TO THE PACKER.

BAKING.

WEIGHING & PACKING FOR DELIVERY.

GATHERING BAKED MATZOTH.

The Modern Making of Matzah 1908

מַצָּה זוּ שֶׁאָנוּ אוֹכְלִים עַל שׁוּם מָה. עַל
שׁוּם שֶׁלֹּא הִסְפִּיק בְּצֵקָם שֶׁל אֲבוֹתֵינוּ לְהַחֲמִיץ
עַד שֶׁנִּגְלָה עֲלֵיהֶם מֶלֶךְ מַלְכֵי הַמְּלָכִים
הַקָּדוֹשׁ בָּרוּךְ הוּא וּגְאָלָם. שֶׁנֶּאֱמַר וַיֹּאפוּ
אֶת־הַבָּצֵק אֲשֶׁר הוֹצִיאוּ מִמִּצְרַיִם עֻגֹת מַצּוֹת
כִּי לֹא חָמֵץ כִּי־גֹרְשׁוּ מִמִּצְרַיִם וְלֹא יָכְלוּ
לְהִתְמַהְמֵהַּ וְגַם־צֵדָה לֹא־עָשׂוּ לָהֶם:
מָרוֹר זֶה שֶׁאָנוּ אוֹכְלִים עַל שׁוּם מָה. עַל שׁוּם
שֶׁמֵּרְרוּ הַמִּצְרִים אֶת חַיֵּי אֲבוֹתֵינוּ בְּמִצְרָיִם.
שֶׁנֶּאֱמַר וַיְמָרְרוּ אֶת־חַיֵּיהֶם בַּעֲבֹדָה קָשָׁה
בְּחֹמֶר וּבִלְבֵנִים וּבְכָל־עֲבֹדָה בַּשָּׂדֶה אֵת כָּל־
עֲבֹדָתָם אֲשֶׁר־עָבְדוּ בָהֶם בְּפָרֶךְ:

**Mark Weinberg Draws
a Matzah Bakery on the
East Side of New York in 1908**

The matzah bakery seen on the
opposite page was one of the busiest
in the New York area. Located in a
tenement house, it produced two
million pounds of matzah in 1908.

On the first floor, a large machine
ground meal made from the cracked
and broken remnants of matzah. The
grinding and the constant preparation
of flour throughout the building
covered all the workers with "a white
mist of floating flour." The processes of
kneading the dough, cutting it into
manageable pieces, perforating it with
a small spiked wheel and then slicing it
into squares for baking were done with
great precision.

Artist, Mark Weinberg, was noted for his
drawings in the *Jewish Chronicle* and
Jewish World of London. In 1907 he
moved to the USA. Only two of his
drawings have survived, the matzah
factory of 1908 and a family seder
scene of 1909.

The drawing is found in
American Hebrew April 17,1908

Point to the matzot and say:

This Matzah that we eat —what is the reason for it?
Because the dough of our ancestors had not yet
leavened when the King of Kings, the Blessed Holy
One, revealed Himself to them and redeemed them,
as said: "And the dough they had brought along out
of Egypt they baked into unleavened cakes, for there
was no leaven, because they had been driven out of
Egypt and had had no time to tarry; they had not
even prepared any provisions for themselves."

(Exodus 12:39)

Point to the bitter herbs and say:

This Bitter Herb that we eat — what is the reason for
it? Because the Egyptians embittered the lives of our
ancestors in Egypt, as said: "They embittered their
lives with hard labor at clay and brick-making, and
all sorts of work in the fields — with all the tasks at
which they ruthlessly worked them." (Exodus 1:14)

**21,000 miles of matzah
in USA in 1950**

Macy's, which has the largest Passover
food department in the country, stocks
four brands of matzah, ranging in price
from 24 cents for 12 ounces to $1.24 for
five pounds. In the USA this year
12,000,000 pounds of matzah will be
consumed. If laid one next to another
it would stretch 21,000 miles.

New York Times. March 23, 1950

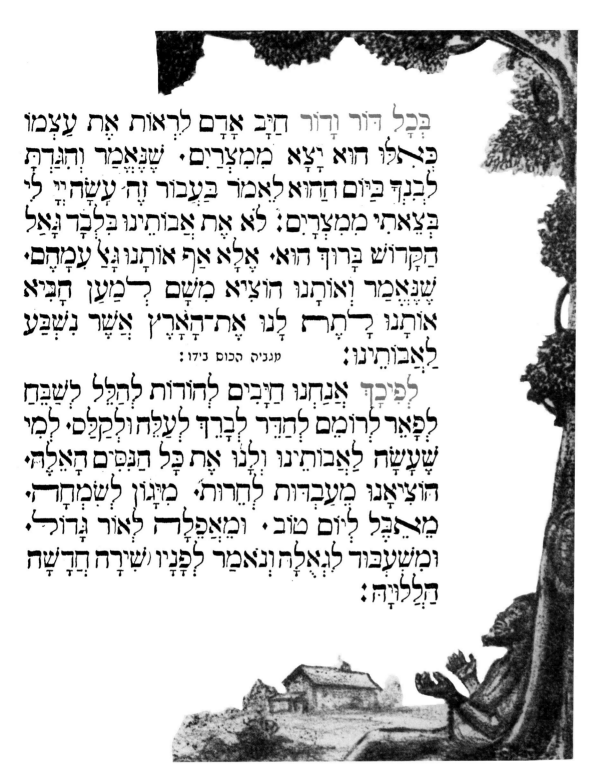

בְּכָל דּוֹר וָדוֹר חַיָּב אָדָם לִרְאוֹת אֶת עַצְמוֹ כְּאִלּוּ הוּא יָצָא מִמִּצְרַיִם. שֶׁנֶּאֱמַר וְהִגַּדְתָּ לְבִנְךָ בַּיּוֹם הַהוּא לֵאמֹר בַּעֲבוּר זֶה עָשָׂה יְיָ לִי בְּצֵאתִי מִמִּצְרָיִם: לֹא אֶת אֲבוֹתֵינוּ בִּלְבָד גָּאַל הַקָּדוֹשׁ בָּרוּךְ הוּא. אֶלָּא אַף אוֹתָנוּ גָּאַל עִמָּהֶם. שֶׁנֶּאֱמַר וְאוֹתָנוּ הוֹצִיא מִשָּׁם לְמַעַן הָבִיא אוֹתָנוּ לָתֶת לָנוּ אֶת־הָאָרֶץ אֲשֶׁר נִשְׁבַּע לַאֲבוֹתֵינוּ:

מגביה הכוס בידו:

לְפִיכָךְ אֲנַחְנוּ חַיָּבִים לְהוֹדוֹת לְהַלֵּל לְשַׁבֵּחַ לְפָאֵר לְרוֹמֵם לְהַדֵּר לְבָרֵךְ לְעַלֵּה וּלְקַלֵּס. לְמִי שֶׁעָשָׂה לַאֲבוֹתֵינוּ וְלָנוּ אֶת כָּל הַנִּסִּים הָאֵלֶּה. הוֹצִיאָנוּ מֵעַבְדוּת לְחֵרוּת. מִיָּגוֹן לְשִׂמְחָה. מֵאֵבֶל לְיוֹם טוֹב. וּמֵאֲפֵלָה לְאוֹר גָּדוֹל. וּמִשִּׁעְבּוּד לִגְאֻלָּה וְנֹאמַר לְפָנָיו שִׁירָה חֲדָשָׁה הַלְלוּיָהּ:

Haggadah for Young American Jews prepared by Isadore Krakower (Philadelphia, 1951) illustrated by Freda Leibovitz Reiter.
In his introduction Krakower writes: "Pesach teaches us that freedom is a priceless gift, and that we deserve to be free only if we are brave and help one another to secure and preserve freedom."

From Slavery to Freedom

The real story of our nation begins with the eager rush from slavery to freedom; and the far-off event remains unforgotten because we have not attained to our ideal. And if in the manifold desires, aspirations and ideals which have formed the Jewish people, we can find an overmastering passion which we can claim as our mundane mission, it is the eternal quest for freedom.

We have participated in all the enfranchising struggles; and today so many Jews are to be found in the ranks of progressive and fadidist politics because to the Jew life means freedom. And the world which has eaten the bread of our thought and the salt of our brains in its quest for freedom, has denied us it. Today even the Russian constitutional movement, for which so many Jews have sacrificed their careers, promises the Jew if it succeeds - nothing. And we still adopt the policy of the "Open Door!"

Maccabaean, March, 1904

In every generation, every person is to consider himself as having personally come out of Egypt. As said: "And you shall tell your son on that day, saying: This commemorates what God did for me when I went out of Egypt." (Exodus 13:8) For the Blessed Holy One did not redeem our ancestors alone; He also redeemed us along with them, as written: "And He brought us out of there, in order to take us to give us the land concerning which He had made a vow to our ancestors." (Deuteronomy 6:23)

Raise the cup of wine, cover the matzot, and say:

That is why we are duty bound to thank, praise, laud, glorify, exalt, extol, bless, acclaim and adore Him Who performed all these wonders for our ancestors and us: He brought us from slavery to freedom, from sorrow to joy, from mourning to holiday, and from darkness to great light, and from bondage to redemption. So let us declaim a new song to Him. Halleluiah.

The Board of Jewish Education of
Chicago issued songbooks for each of
the holidays under the guidance of its
musical director Harry Coopersmith.
Little Book of Jewish Songs
Chicago, 1934
Anna and Louis Geffen Collection

מניח הכום ומגלה הטלות במקדס :

הַלְלוּיָהּ הַלְלוּ עַבְדֵי יְיָ הַלְלוּ אֶת־שֵׁם יְיָ:
יְהִי שֵׁם יְיָ מְבֹרָךְ מֵעַתָּה וְעַד־עוֹלָם: מִמִּזְרַח־
שֶׁמֶשׁ עַד־מְבוֹאוֹ מְהֻלָּל שֵׁם יְיָ: רָם עַל־כָּל־
גּוֹיִם יְיָ עַל־הַשָּׁמַיִם כְּבוֹדוֹ: מִי כַּיְיָ אֱלֹהֵינוּ
הַמַּגְבִּיהִי לָשָׁבֶת: הַמַּשְׁפִּילִי לִרְאוֹת בַּשָּׁמַיִם
וּבָאָרֶץ: מְקִימִי מֵעָפָר דָּל מֵאַשְׁפֹּת יָרִים אֶבְיוֹן:
לְהוֹשִׁיבִי עִם־נְדִיבִים עִם נְדִיבֵי עַמּוֹ: מוֹשִׁיבִי
עֲקֶרֶת הַבַּיִת אֵם־הַבָּנִים שְׂמֵחָה הַלְלוּיָהּ:

בְּצֵאת יִשְׂרָאֵל מִמִּצְרָיִם בֵּית יַעֲקֹב מֵעַם
לֹעֵז: הָיְתָה יְהוּדָה לְקָדְשׁוֹ יִשְׂרָאֵל
מַמְשְׁלוֹתָיו· הַיָּם רָאָה וַיָּנֹס הַיַּרְדֵּן יִסֹּב לְאָחוֹר:
הֶהָרִים רָקְדוּ כְאֵילִים גְּבָעוֹת כִּבְנֵי־צֹאן:
מַה־לְּךָ הַיָּם כִּי תָנוּם הַיַּרְדֵּן תִּסֹּב לְאָחוֹר·
הֶהָרִים תִּרְקְדוּ כְאֵילִים גְּבָעוֹת כִּבְנֵי־צֹאן·
מִלְּפְנֵי אָדוֹן חוּלִי אָרֶץ מִלְּפְנֵי אֱלוֹהַּ יַעֲקֹב·
הַהֹפְכִי הַצּוּר אֲגַם־מָיִם חַלָּמִישׁ לְמַעְיְנוֹ־
מָיִם:

Leaving Egypt - American Style

In this 1921 circular the State Bank introduced the concept of
a Passover Club, weekly savings throughout the year which
insured funds to buy food and clothing for the holiday.

Put down the cup and uncover the matzot

Halleluiah.

Praise — O God's servants — praise the Name of God. Blessed be the Name of God now and forever. From the sun's rising-place to its setting-place let the Name of God be praised. High above all the nations is God, our God: enthroned so high yet deigning to look so low; raising the wretched out of the dust, lifting the poor off the dungheap, to give them a place among the high and mighty — among the high and mighty of His people; making the barren recluse a happy mother of children. Halleluiah. (Psalm 113)

When Israel came out of Egypt, the House of Jacob from a strange-languaged people —
Judah became His sanctuary, Israel His dominion.
The sea saw and fled; the Jordan turned back.
The mountains skipped like rams,
the hills like young sheep.
What is it, sea; why do you run?
Jordan — why do you turn back?
Why, mountains, do you skip like rams,
you hills like young sheep?
Dance, earth, when the Lord appears,
when Jacob's God shows,
Who turned the rock into a pool of water,
the flintrock into a gushing fountain!
(Psalms 114)

בָּרוּךְ אַתָּה יְיָ אֱלֹהֵינוּ מֶלֶךְ הָעוֹלָם · אֲשֶׁר
גְּאָלָנוּ וְגָאַל אֶת אֲבוֹתֵינוּ מִמִּצְרַיִם וְהִגִּיעָנוּ
לַלַּיְלָה הַזֶּה לֶאֱכָל בּוֹ מַצָּה וּמָרוֹר: כֵּן יְיָ אֱלֹהֵינוּ
וֵאלֹהֵי אֲבוֹתֵינוּ יַגִּיעֵנוּ לְמוֹעֲדִים וְלִרְגָלִים אֲחֵרִים
הַבָּאִים לִקְרָאתֵנוּ לְשָׁלוֹם שְׂמֵחִים בְּבִנְיַן עִירֶךָ
וְשָׂשִׂים בַּעֲבוֹדָתֶךָ · וְנֹאכַל שָׁם מִן הַזְּבָחִים
וּמִן הַפְּסָחִים אֲשֶׁר יַגִּיעַ דָּמָם עַל קִיר מִזְבַּחֲךָ
לְרָצוֹן · וְנוֹדֶה לְךָ שִׁיר חָדָשׁ עַל גְּאֻלָּתֵנוּ וְעַל
פְּדוּת נַפְשֵׁנוּ · בָּרוּךְ אַתָּה יְיָ גָּאַל יִשְׂרָאֵל:
בָּרוּךְ אַתָּה יְיָ אֱלֹהֵינוּ מֶלֶךְ הָעוֹלָם בּוֹרֵא
פְּרִי הַגָּפֶן: וְשׁוֹתִין נִהְסִיבַת שְׂמֹאל:

The Train Seder

In April 1919 a seder was held in a pullman car on a siding in the railroad yards in Detroit, Michigan. Soldiers, returning from Europe, were on their way to Camp Grant, near Chicago, Illinois to be discharged. When it was realized that they could not get to Illinois in time for the beginning of Passover, the Jewish Welfare Board arranged a seder for them on the train route and obtained a rabbi to officiate.

Jewish Welfare Board in World War I
New York, 1920

All the participants lift their cups of wine, and say:

Be blessed, God, our god, King of the universe, Who redeemed us and redeemed our ancestors from Egypt, and enabled us to live to this night to eat matzah and bitter herbs. In the same way, God, our god and god of our ancestors, let us live until the other set-times and festivals approach us — let us reach them in peace, rejoicing in the rebuilding of Your city and delighting in the performance of Your service, and partaking of the sacrifices and the Passover offerings whose blood shall reach the walls of Your altar propitiously, and we will thank You with a new song for our redemption and the emancipation of our souls. Be blessed, God, Who redeemed Israel.

Say the following blessing and drink the second cup, reclining.

Be blessed, God, our god, King of the universe — creator of the vine.

Mr. and Mrs. William Silver of Atlanta, Georgia, host at their seder during World War I, Jewish soldiers stationed at nearby military installations. American patriotism is resplendent in the flags which serve as the background. The seder was held on March 28, 1918 at 328 Central Avenue in Atlanta.

William E. Silver collection

רָחְצָה

וְאַחַר כָּךְ נוֹטְלִים יְדֵיהֶם וּמְבָרְכִים

בָּרוּךְ אַתָּה יְיָ אֱלֹהֵינוּ מֶלֶךְ הָעוֹלָם אֲשֶׁר קִדְּשָׁנוּ בְּמִצְוֹתָיו וְצִוָּנוּ עַל נְטִילַת יָדָיִם:

מוֹצִיא מַצָּה

אוֹחֵז בְּיָדוֹ ג' הַמַּצוֹת עִם הַפְּרוּסָה שְׁבֵּינֵיהֶם וּמְבָרֵךְ הַמּוֹצִיא וְעַל אֲכִילַת מַצָּה וְבוֹלֵעַ מֵהָעֶלְיוֹנָה כַּזַּיִת וּמֵהַפְּרוּסָה ג"כ כַּזַּיִת וְאוֹכְלָם בְּיַחַד.

בָּרוּךְ אַתָּה יְיָ אֱלֹהֵינוּ מֶלֶךְ הָעוֹלָם · הַמּוֹצִיא לֶחֶם מִן הָאָרֶץ:
בָּרוּךְ אַתָּה יְיָ אֱלֹהֵינוּ מֶלֶךְ הָעוֹלָם · אֲשֶׁר קִדְּשָׁנוּ בְּמִצְוֹתָיו וְצִוָּנוּ עַל אֲכִילַת מַצָּה:

Revolutionary War Matzah

Aaron Lopez, a leading Jewish merchant and patriot in Newport, Rhode Island, fled before Passover in 1776 to escape the British troops and went to Portsmouth, Rhode Island. As was his custom, he sent 100 pounds of flour to Newport so matzah could be baked for the community. Hence, the matzah Lopez and his family ate in that year in exile rightly bore the title, "bread of affliction".

Jacob Rader Marcus,
The Colonial Jew: 1492-1776,
Detroit, 1970

How They Make Passover Cakes

New Yorkers having occasion lately to pass through Grand Street, near Broadway, must have noticed a store in which an unusual bustle was manifested, the windows filled with large crackers, curiously punched with numerous holes, signs suspended with mystical characters in Hebrew and English - "Matzoth", and employees running about receiving and executing orders. The noise of machinery proceeded from the cellar and if one were sufficiently adventurous to peer into these lower regions, he would think, judging from the confusion and hurry, that this was an enterprising bakery, using every possible means to fill an immense order, for which there was little time left.

Seven mixings are made in an hour, each mixing taking 28 pounds of flour. This amount is accurately weighed and the water poured upon it carefully noted so that the Matzoth are of equal consistency. After kneading the flour it is "broken".

The dough is placed on a low table in one of the angles of the bakery, and is crushed by a stout beam, which fastened to the table at one end, is sat upon by a workman at the other, who rides it, as it were, in a semicircle back and forth until the dough is considered flattened.

continued on next page

"Riding the matzah dough"
Frank Leslie's
Illustrated Newspaper,
New York, April 10, 1858
Ezra P. Gorodesky collection

continued from previous page

The dough then passes through a series of rollers until the required tenuity is obtained, when it undergoes its last operation prior to being baked, "cutting and ducking" all done by one machine, which cuts it into square or round cakes, as may be desired, and also punches that variety of indentations which gives Matzoth a certain picturesqueness. The bakers proper then use their long wooden shovels with good effect, depositing the soft material in the oven and in a minute drawing it out, converted into crisp agreeable Matzoth.

After baking, the Matzoth are carried into the stock-room where they are packed neatly into boxes, as ordered or are stacked in imposing rows awaiting orders.

In 1831, 50 barrels of flour were used to bake 8000 pounds of Matzoth; all that was needed for New York. In 1847, two bakers Spier and S. Cohen did all the Matzoth preparation. Cohen's trade amounted to 365 barrels of Matzoth from which he supplied Jews in neighboring communities as well.

In 1871, 3000 barrels of Matzoth were needed for New York alone with 1000 more required for families in Canada, and some southern cities, since the large towns have their own bakeries.

New York Times, April 4, 1871

A dozen Jewish bakers supply all the Hebrew families in New York and send to communities all over the USA, Canada and South America. 4000 barrels of flour were used in order to make 650,000 pounds of Matzoth.

New York Times, April 10, 1873

Rahatza

Rinse the hands and say the following blessing:

Be blessed, God, our god, King of the universe, Who has sanctified us by His commandments and commanded us concerning the rinsing of the hands.

Motzi

Pick up the three matzot
from the Seder tray and say the following blessing:

Be blessed, God, our god, King of the universe, Who brings forth bread from the earth.

Matzah

Replace the bottom matzah. Everybody gets a piece of the top and middle matzot. Say the following blessing and eat, reclining.
(Some first dip the matzah in haroset)

Be blessed, God, our God, King of the universe, Who sanctified us with His commandments and commanded us concerning the eating of matzah.

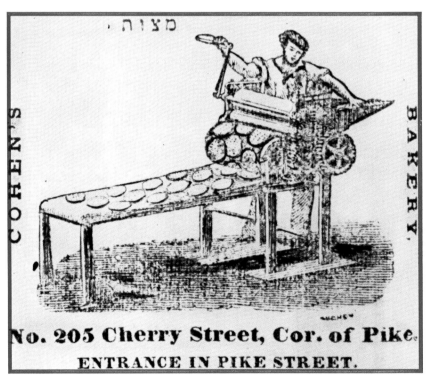

Earliest American Matzah Machine

S.R. Cohen initiated illustrated advertisements of Jewish ritual foods in the USA when this ad appeared in the *Asmonean* weekly newspaper in 1852 in New York. Until 1850, matzah was hand-baked. The matzah machine, shown in this ad, was challenged and a query, "she'elah," was directed to the Chief Rabbi of England, Herman Adler. He wrote a responsum, "teshuva," permitting the use of the machine and from then on most American matzah has been machine baked.

Brocha on the Makror (bitter herbs)

BLESSED ·are You · G-D · OUR G-D · KING · of the WORLD · WHO · HAS MADE us HOLY · WITH HIS COMMANDMENTS · AND COMMANDED · US · ABOUT · EATING · BITTER : · VEGETABLES

"Our Way" Passover brochure in sign language for the Jewish deaf is from a series produced by the National Conference of Synagogue Youth of the Union of Orthodox Jewish Congregations of America.

מָ ר וֹ ר

וְאַחַר כָּךְ יִתֵּן כַּזַּיִת מָרוֹר שְׁקוֹרִין ליטוגא ויטבול בַּחֲרוֹסֶת וּמְנַעֵר הַחֲרוֹסֶת
מֵעָלָיו וְאוֹכְלוֹ בְּלִי הֲסִבָּה, וְטֶרֶם אָכְלוֹ יְבָרֵךְ

בָּרוּךְ אַתָּה יְיָ אֱלֹהֵינוּ מֶלֶךְ הָעוֹלָם· אֲשֶׁר
קִדְּשָׁנוּ בְּמִצְוֹתָיו וְצִוָּנוּ עַל אֲכִילַת מָרוֹר:

כּוֹרֵךְ

וְאַחַ"כ יִקַּח כַּזַּיִת מִן הַמַּצָּה הַתַּחְתּוֹנָה וְכוֹרֵךְ בָּהּ כַּזַּיִת מָרוֹר וְאוֹכְלָם בְּיַחַד
בְּלֹא טִבּוּל וְבְלֹא בְּרָכָה.

זֵכֶר לַמִּקְדָּשׁ כְּהִלֵּל:

כֵּן עָשָׂה הִלֵּל בִּזְמַן שֶׁבֵּית הַמִּקְדָּשׁ קַיָּם· הָיָה
כּוֹרֵךְ (פֶּסַח) מַצָּה וּמָרוֹר וְאוֹכֵל בְּיַחַד· לְקַיֵּם
מַה שֶׁנֶּאֱמַר עַל מַצּוֹת וּמְרוֹרִים יֹאכְלֻהוּ:

שֻׁלְחָן עוֹרֵךְ

וְאַחַר כָּךְ אוֹכְלִים וְשׁוֹתִים לְשׂוֹבַע כְּפֶסַח. כִּיד ה' הַטּוֹבָה עָלֵיהֶס.

Making Haroset in 1739

Congregation Shearith Israel of New York spent 12 shillings and sevenpence in 1739 to prepare haroset and distribute it to all members of the synagogue.

David and Tamar de Sola Pool,
An Old Faith in the New World,
New York, 1955

A GROUP of FRIENDS PERFORMING פסח PASSOVER EVE at H.J.HEPPNER סדר ONE YEAR AFTER THE GREAT DISASTER IN SAN FRANCISCO CAL. U.S.A.

This picture was taken of the Heppner family seder in San Francisco in 1907,
one year after the terrible earthquake there in 1906.
Western Jewish History Center of the Judah L. Magnes Museum, Berkeley, California

American soldiers stand on alert around the seder table on the cover of the Fort Sill, Oklahoma. Chaplain's Bulletin for Passover, April 1966.

Maror

Everybody dips some bitter herb in haroset, says the following blessing, and eats sitting up.

Be blessed, God, our god, King of the universe, Who sanctified us with His commandments and commanded us concerning the eating of maror.

Korech

Using the bottom matzah from the tray, everybody makes a maror sandwich, says the following passage, and eats reclining.

In remembrance of the Temple, according to Hillel the Elder. This is what Hillel did when the Temple was standing: he would wrap together the portion of the Paschal offering, the matzah and the maror and eat them together, in order to do what is said: "On matzot and bitter herbs they shall eat it." (Numbers 9:11)

Shulhan Orech

Remove the Seder tray from the table and eat the festival meal.

Finding the Afikoman is one of the features of the seder, as depicted in this drawing from the Waldbaum's Passover Circular 1990. When colored, it could be submitted as an entry in the store's Passover competition. Gift certificates were awarded to the winners.

American Jewish Archives
Cincinnati, Ohio

THIS CERTIFIES THAT
_____

IS

Champion
Afikoman finder

_____
Date

_____
Master Afikoman Hides

Chaplain Geoffrey D. Botnick of the
U. S. Navy prepared this "afikoman finder"
certificate for the sedarim held at the Naval
Training Center, Great Lakes, Illinois in
March 1975.

American Jewish Archives, Cincinnati, Ohio

צָפוּן

ולאחר הסעודה יקח הפרוסה שהטמין ויאכל ממנו כזית לאפיקומן ויתן לכל
אחד ואחד.

Tzafun

Put the tray back on table, give everybody a piece of matzah
from the large section put away for the Afikoman, say the following
passage, and eat reclining.

(In remembrance of the Passover Offering, eaten
after satiation.)

TOURO SYNAGOGUE

DEDICATED 1763
OLDEST SYNAGOGUE IN
AMERICA. DESIGNATED A
NATIONAL HISTORIC SITE
1946

"... to bigotry no sanction,
to persecution no assistance ..."
G. WASHINGTON – 1790

Official First Day Cover approved by Touro Synagogue

© 1981 Society of Friends of Touro Synagogue

MAY 1759
NEW YORK

Conformable to your desire a נדבה was made in our Synagogue the Seventh day of פסח , when a contribution of £149,6 was offered towards building at Newport a place of worship.

PARNAS
SHEARITH ISRAEL SYNAGOGUE

①

② *First Hebrew map of Palestine (Eretz Yisrael) printed in USA, New York 1840*

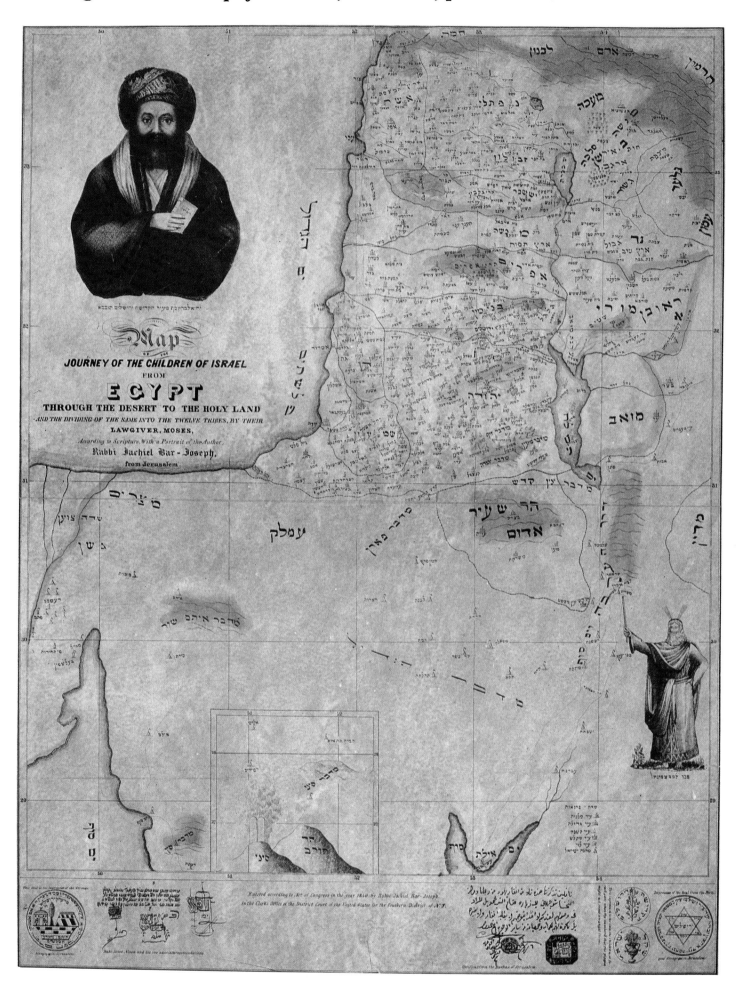

③ The Seder

Meichel Pressman (1864-1953), New York, 1950. Watercolor on paper. *The Jewish Museum, New York*

④ *Family Seder Plate by Ilya Schor - 1956*

The Gulf War

Passover Seder
U.S. Military Personnel, 1991/5751
Princess Cunard Ship
Bahrain and Saudi Arabia

6

7

8

9

10

11

12

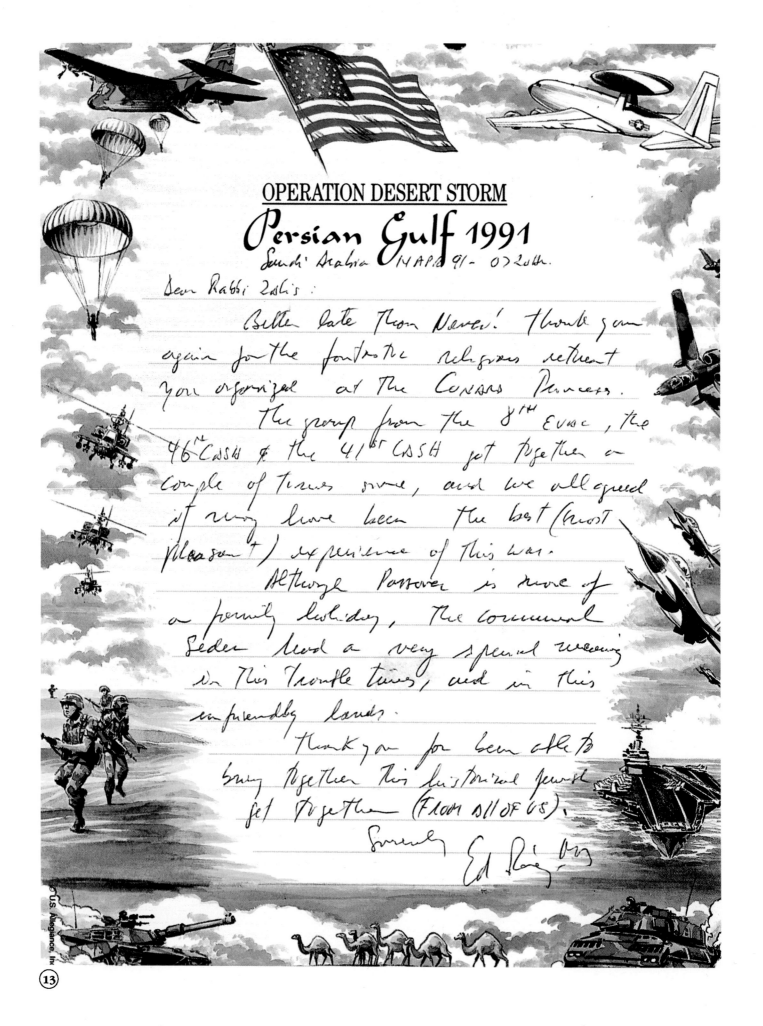

OPERATION DESERT STORM

Persian Gulf 1991

Saudi Arabia 14 APRIL 91 - 0720 hr.

Dear Rabbi Zalis:

Better late Than Never! Thank you again for the fantastic religious retreat you organized at The Cunard Princess.

The group from the 8TH Evac, the 46th CASH & the 41st CASH got together a couple of times since, and we all agreed it may have been the best (most pleasant) experience of This war.

Although Passover is more of a family holiday, The communal Seder had a very special meaning in This Trouble times, and in This unfriendly lands.

Thank you for been able To bring together This historical Jewish get Together (FROM ALL OF US).

Sincerely
Ed Ring Ong

Seder Plate *by Carol Brull*
Courtesy of Galerie Robin, Nashville, Tennessee

Seder Plate and Goblet *by R. Lipnick*
Courtesy of In the Spirit Gallery, New York

Color Plates

1 Dedicated in 1763, the Touro Synagogue in Newport, Rhode Island, is the oldest synagogue building in the United States and was depicted on an American stamp in 1982. On Passover in 1759, an appeal for funds for the construction of the Newport synagogue was held at Congregation Shearith Israel in New York. The original letter is at the *American Jewish Historical Society,*
Waltham, Massachusetts.

2 The 1695 Amsterdam Haggadah was the first to include a Hebrew map of Eretz Yisrael (Palestine). The map depicted here is the first Hebrew map of Palestine printed in the U.S.A., and the original is in the Library of Congress. Jachiel Bar-Joseph, a Jerusalem emissary visiting New York from 1839 until 1840, issued the map in conjunction with the G. Endicott Lithograph firm of New York. The map measures 24 x 36 inches and was printed in black and white. Bar-Joseph placed his own picture on the map, failing to take note of its real author, Rabbi Yehoseph Schwarz, who produced the original map in Trieste, Italy in 1832. The tribal divisions of the country as well as Goshen, Egypt, Mt. Sinai, the Sinai desert and the Reed Sea are all seen, with Moses' staff pointing to the north. The color reproduction was created by Mr. Chemi Burg of Rehovot, Israel (© Chemi Burg).

3 The Seder by Meichel Pressman (1864-1953) is a watercolor on paper. Pressman had begun to draw at age 84, and in this work, he recreates the Passover of his youth in Poland. The depiction of the two golden candelabra is repeated by the twin trees. Around the clock are the Hebrew words from the Haggadah — "Next year in Jerusalem." The painting was included in the exhibit, "The Jewish Heritage in American Folk Art," held at the Jewish Museum in New York in 1984.
Jewish Museum, New York

4 Frieda and J. Max Abramowitz of Baltimore, Maryland commissioned Ilya Schor to make a Seder plate for them in 1956. Schor fashioned the plate in silver, etching into it his delicate drawings of Seder scenes. He engraved on the plate the names of the Abramowitz family members. Since Schor executed only a few pieces of this type, the family loaned the plate for the retrospective exhibit in Schor's memory held at the Jewish Museum in 1965.
Frieda and J. Max Abramowitz collection
loaned by Irving Abramowitz, Jerusalem

5 The Barton's Candy Company sold metal containers with a "Historic Seder Plate Assortment" of chocolates as a "family memento" in the early 1950s. Issued in 1953, this painted tin top has a depiction of all the steps of the Seder in its circular border.
Anna and Louis Geffen collection Atlanta, Georgia

6 During the Gulf War in 1991, the U.S. rented the Cunard Princess ship in Bahrain harbor and used it as a locale for troops on leave. Chaplain David Zalis of the U.S. Army arranged for Sedarim for Jewish military personnel to be held on the ship. A Passover retreat, March 28-31, 1991, included the search for and burning of leaven, the Sedarim, services and classes. Four hundred soldiers, marines and air force personnel participated.
The photographs from the Gulf War
are courtesy of Chaplain David Zalis, Jerusalem.

7 Chaplain David Zalis gives matzah to a Kuwaiti lad in the desert.

8 It took two to carry an arriving crate of matzah.

9 A Torah was flown in from a U.S. military base in Germany for the Passover services on the Cunard Princess. When the Torah arrived in the Persian Gulf, it was directed to the wrong military airport but was eventually found. On the eve of Passover, Chaplain David Zalis brought the Torah onto the ship under the traditional marriage canopy.

10 Waiters on the Cunard Princess help prepare the tables for the Seder.

11 Arriving just in time for the Seder, these two soldiers enjoyed this festival of freedom.

12 Chaplain David Zalis and General Norman H. Schwarzkopf.

13 This letter is representative of the feelings of those who participated in the Sedarim on the Cunard Princess. The illustrations on the stationery depict aspects of the Persian Gulf campaign.

14 The Seder Plate by Carol Brull is an abstract ceramic plate with the Reed Sea on the left and Israel as a free nation on the right. The figures on the plate represent the Jews crossing the desert and each one holds one of the symbolic foods placed on the Seder plate.
Courtesy of Galerie Robin, Nashville , Tennessee.

15 Seder Plate and Elijah Cup by Robert Lipnick. The vivid colors of this ceramic plate and cup evoke the themes of spring and freedom, epitomized by Passover.
Courtesy of In the Spirit Gallery, New York.

שִׁיר הַמַּעֲלוֹת, בְּשׁוּב יְיָ, אֶת שִׁיבַת צִיּוֹן, הָיִינוּ כְּחֹלְמִים: אָז יִמָּלֵא שְׂחוֹק פִּינוּ וּלְשׁוֹנֵנוּ רִנָּה, אָז יֹאמְרוּ בַגּוֹיִם, הִגְדִּיל יְיָ לַעֲשׂוֹת עִם אֵלֶּה: הִגְדִּיל יְיָ לַעֲשׂוֹת עִמָּנוּ, הָיִינוּ שְׂמֵחִים: שׁוּבָה יְיָ אֶת שְׁבִיתֵנוּ, כַּאֲפִיקִים בַּנֶּגֶב: הַזֹּרְעִים בְּדִמְעָה בְּרִנָּה יִקְצֹרוּ: הָלוֹךְ יֵלֵךְ וּבָכֹה נֹשֵׂא מֶשֶׁךְ הַזָּרַע, בֹּא יָבֹא בְרִנָּה, נֹשֵׂא אֲלֻמֹּתָיו:

בָּרֵךְ

וּמְבָרֵךְ בִּרְכַּת הַמָּזוֹן.

שְׁלֹשָׁה שֶׁאָכְלוּ כְּאַחַת חַיָּבִין בְּזִמּוּן כֵּיצַד מְזַמְּנִים?

הַמְזַמֵּן אוֹמֵר*הַב לָן וְנִבָרֵךְ, וְהֵם עוֹנִים יְהִי שֵׁם יְיָ מְבוֹרָךְ מֵעַתָּה וְעַד עוֹלָם: וְהַמְזַמֵּן אוֹמֵר בִּרְשׁוּת ≈ ≈ נְבָרֵךְ (נעשרה מוסיף אֱלֹהֵינוּ) שֶׁאָכַלְנוּ מִשֶּׁלּוֹ: וְהַמְסוּבִין עוֹנִים בָּרוּךְ (נעשרה מוסיפין אֱלֹהֵינוּ) שֶׁאָכַלְנוּ מִשֶּׁלּוֹ וּבְטוּבוֹ חָיִינוּ: וְכָל הָעוֹמְדִי׳ שָׁם אַף שָׁאֵינָם מִן הַמְסוּבִין

(וְּאִם הֵם יַעֲנוּ וַיֹאמְרוּ בָּרוּךְ וּמְבוֹרָךְ שְׁמוֹ תָּמִיד לְעוֹלָם וָעֶד:)

וְחוֹזֵר הַמְזַמֵּן וְאוֹמֵר בָּרוּךְ (אֱלֹהֵינוּ) שֶׁאָכַלְנוּ מִשֶּׁלּוֹ וּבְטוּבוֹ חָיִינוּ: בָּרוּךְ הוּא וּבָרוּךְ שְׁמוֹ:

Barech

Fill the third cup

Shir Hamaalot:

When God restored Zion's fortune, we were like people restored to health.

Our mouths were filled with laughter then, our tongues with joyous song.

The word went round among the nations: "God has done great things for them!"

God indeed did great things for us, and we rejoiced.

Restore, O God, our fortunes, like the torrents filling the wadis in the south.

Those who sow in tears shall reap with joyous song.

Though he goes along weeping — the man carrying the seed bag — he shall come back singing joyously as he carries home his sheaves. (Psalm 126)

If at least three males past Bar Mitzvah are present, the person conducting the Seder or a male appointed by him lifts his cup of wine and leads the saying of Grace-after-Meals.

Leader: My masters, let us bless.
Others: Let God's Name be blessed now and forever.
Leader: Let God's Name be blessed now and forever. By permission of (the host and of) our masters and my teachers, let us bless Him (if ten male past Bar Mitzvah are present say "our god" instead of "Him") of Whose fare we have eaten.
Others: Blessed be Him (or, if ten adult males are present, "our god") of Whose fare we have eaten and on Whose bounty we live.
Leader: Blessed be Him (or, if ten adult males are present, "our god") of Whose fare we have eaten and on Whose bounty we live.

All say:

Be blessed, God, our god, King of the universe, Who feeds the entire world of His bounty — with grace, with lovingkindness, mercifully. He gives food to all flesh, for His lovingkindness is eternal. And because of His great goodness we have never lacked food, and may we never lack it. For His great Name's sake — for He is a God Who feeds and provides for all, and is good to all, and prepares food for all His creatures that He has created. Be blessed, God, Who feeds all.

We thank You, God, our god, for allotting to our ancestors a desirable, goodly and ample land, and for bringing us out of the land of Egypt, for emancipating us from a land of slavery, for sealing Your covenant in our flesh, for teaching us Your Torah, for making Your statutes known to us, for bestowing life, grace and lovingkindness upon us, and for feeding us and supplying us with food continually, every day, at all times, and at every hour.

For all this, God, our god, we thank You and bless You. May Your Name be blessed by every living thing always, forever. As written: "When you have eaten your fill, you shall bless God, your god, for the goodly land He has given you." (Deuteronomy 8:10) Be blessed, God, for the land and for the food (in the Land of Israel, say "its food").

בָּרוּךְ אַתָּה יְיָ אֱלֹהֵינוּ מֶלֶךְ הָעוֹלָם הַזָּן אֶת הָעוֹלָם כֻּלּוֹ בְּטוּבוֹ בְּחֵן בְּחֶסֶד וּבְרַחֲמִים הוּא נוֹתֵן לֶחֶם לְכָל בָּשָׂר כִּי לְעוֹלָם חַסְדּוֹ: וּבְטוּבוֹ הַגָּדוֹל תָּמִיד לֹא חָסַר לָנוּ וְאַל יֶחְסַר לָנוּ מָזוֹן לְעוֹלָם וָעֶד: בַּעֲבוּר שְׁמוֹ הַגָּדוֹל כִּי הוּא זָן וּמְפַרְנֵס לַכֹּל וּמֵטִיב לַכֹּל וּמֵכִין מָזוֹן לְכָל בְּרִיּוֹתָיו אֲשֶׁר בָּרָא בָּרוּךְ אַתָּה יְיָ הַזָּן אֶת הַכֹּל:

נוֹדֶה לְּךָ יְיָ אֱלֹהֵינוּ עַל שֶׁהִנְחַלְתָּ לַאֲבוֹתֵינוּ אֶרֶץ חֶמְדָּה טוֹבָה וּרְחָבָה וְעַל שֶׁהוֹצֵאתָנוּ יְיָ אֱלֹהֵינוּ מֵאֶרֶץ מִצְרַיִם וּפְדִיתָנוּ מִבֵּית עֲבָדִים וְעַל בְּרִיתְךָ שֶׁחָתַמְתָּ בִּבְשָׂרֵנוּ וְעַל תּוֹרָתְךָ שֶׁלִּמַּדְתָּנוּ וְעַל חֻקֶּיךָ שֶׁהוֹדַעְתָּנוּ וְעַל חַיִּים חֵן וָחֶסֶד שֶׁחוֹנַנְתָּנוּ וְעַל אֲכִילַת מָזוֹן שָׁאַתָּה זָן וּמְפַרְנֵס אוֹתָנוּ תָּמִיד בְּכָל יוֹם וּבְכָל עֵת וּבְכָל שָׁעָה:

וְעַל הַכֹּל יְיָ אֱלֹהֵינוּ אֲנַחְנוּ מוֹדִים לָךְ וּמְבָרְכִים אוֹתָךְ יִתְבָּרַךְ שִׁמְךָ בְּפִי כָּל חַי תָּמִיד לְעוֹלָם וָעֶד: כַּכָּתוּב וְאָכַלְתָּ וְשָׂבָעְתָּ וּבֵרַכְתָּ אֶת יְיָ אֱלֹהֶיךָ עַל הָאָרֶץ הַטֹּבָה אֲשֶׁר נָתַן לָךְ • בָּרוּךְ אַתָּה יְיָ עַל הָאָרֶץ וְעַל הַמָּזוֹן:

רַחֵם יְיָ אֱלֹהֵינוּ עַל־יִשְׂרָאֵל עַמֶּךָ וְעַל יְרוּשָׁלַיִם עִירֶךָ וְעַל צִיּוֹן מִשְׁכַּן כְּבוֹדֶךָ וְעַל מַלְכוּת בֵּית דָּוִד מְשִׁיחֶךָ וְעַל הַבַּיִת הַגָּדוֹל וְהַקָּדוֹשׁ שֶׁנִּקְרָא שִׁמְךָ עָלָיו: אֱלֹהֵינוּ אָבִינוּ רְעֵנוּ זוּנֵנוּ פַּרְנְסֵנוּ וְכַלְכְּלֵנוּ וְהַרְוִיחֵנוּ וְהַרְוַח לָנוּ יְיָ אֱלֹהֵינוּ מְהֵרָה מִכָּל צָרוֹתֵינוּ: וְנָא אַל תַּצְרִיכֵנוּ יְיָ אֱלֹהֵינוּ לֹא לִידֵי מַתְּנַת בָּשָׂר וָדָם וְלֹא לִידֵי הַלְוָאָתָם כִּי אִם לְיָדְךָ הַמְּלֵאָה הַפְּתוּחָה הַקְּדוֹשָׁה וְהָרְחָבָה שֶׁלֹּא נֵבוֹשׁ וְלֹא נִכָּלֵם לְעוֹלָם וָעֶד:

ל ש כ ת׳
רְצֵה וְהַחֲלִיצֵנוּ יְיָ אֱלֹהֵינוּ בְּמִצְוֹתֶיךָ וּבְמִצְוַת יוֹם הַשְּׁבִיעִי הַשַּׁבָּת הַגָּדוֹל וְהַקָּדוֹשׁ הַזֶּה כִּי יוֹם זֶה גָּדוֹל וְקָדוֹשׁ הוּא לְפָנֶיךָ לִשְׁבָּת בּוֹ וְלָנוּחַ בּוֹ בְּאַהֲבָה כְּמִצְוַת רְצוֹנֶךָ בִּרְצוֹנְךָ הָנִיחַ לָנוּ יְיָ אֱלֹהֵינוּ שֶׁלֹּא תְהֵי צָרָה וְיָגוֹן וַאֲנָחָה בְּיוֹם מְנוּחָתֵנוּ וְהַרְאֵנוּ יְיָ אֱלֹהֵינוּ בְּנֶחָמַת צִיּוֹן עִירֶךָ וּבְבִנְיַן יְרוּשָׁלַיִם עִיר קָדְשֶׁךָ כִּי אַתָּה הוּא בַּעַל הַיְשׁוּעוֹת וּבַעַל הַנֶּחָמוֹת:

אֱלֹהֵינוּ וֵאלֹהֵי אֲבוֹתֵינוּ יַעֲלֶה וְיָבֹא וְיַגִּיעַ וְיֵרָאֶה וְיֵרָצֶה וְיִשָּׁמַע וְיִפָּקֵד וְיִזָּכֵר זִכְרוֹנֵנוּ וּפִקְדוֹנֵנוּ וְזִכְרוֹן אֲבוֹתֵינוּ וְזִכְרוֹן מָשִׁיחַ בֶּן דָּוִד עַבְדֶּךָ וְזִכְרוֹן יְרוּשָׁלַיִם עִיר קָדְשֶׁךָ וְזִכְרוֹן כָּל־עַמְּךָ בֵּית יִשְׂרָאֵל לְפָנֶיךָ לִפְלֵיטָה לְטוֹבָה לְחֵן וּלְחֶסֶד וּלְרַחֲמִים לְחַיִּים וּלְשָׁלוֹם בְּיוֹם חַג הַמַּצּוֹת הַזֶּה זָכְרֵנוּ יְיָ אֱלֹהֵינוּ בּוֹ לְטוֹבָה וּפָקְדֵנוּ בוֹ לִבְרָכָה וְהוֹשִׁיעֵנוּ בוֹ לְחַיִּים. וּבִדְבַר יְשׁוּעָה וְרַחֲמִים. חוּס וְחָנֵּנוּ וְרַחֵם עָלֵינוּ וְהוֹשִׁיעֵנוּ כִּי אֵלֶיךָ עֵינֵינוּ. כִּי אֵל מֶלֶךְ חַנּוּן וְרַחוּם אָתָּה:

Have mercy, God, our god, on Israel Your people, on Jerusalem Your city, on Zion the dwelling place of Your glory, on the kingdom of the House of David Your anointed one, and on the great and holy house that is called by Your Name. Our God, our Father, our Shepherd — pasture us, feed us, provide for us, and sustain us, and give us relief — and give us speedy relief, God, our god, from all our troubles. Do not, we beg You, God, our god, cause us to become dependent on the handouts of flesh and blood or on their loans, but only on Your hand — full, open, bountiful and generous — so that we shall never be ashamed or be put to shame.

If Passover falls on Shabbat, say the following passage.

Let it be Your will, God, our god, that we shall be strengthened by performing Your commandments — especially by observing this seventh day, this great and holy Sabbath, for this day is great and holy before You, to pause and rest on it lovingly as it was Your pleasure to command. and let it be your will, God, our god, that there shall be no cause for trouble, sorrow or sighing on our day of rest. And show us, God, our god, Zion Your city comforted and Jerusalem Your holy city rebuilt, for You are the giver of salvation and the giver of consolation.

Our God and god of our fathers: let the remembrance and mindfulness of us, the remembrance of our ancestors, the remembrance of Jerusalem Your holy city, and the remembrance of Your entire people the House of Israel come to You, reach You, be seen by You, be favored by You, be heard by You, minded by You and remembered by You to our relief, to our benefit, for grace, for lovingkindness and for mercy, for life and for peace, on this Matzot Festival Day. On this day, God, our god, remember us for good, be mindful of us on it for blessing, and preserve us on it for a good life. And be so merciful as to grace us with the promise of salvation and mercy, and have mercy on us and save us. For to You our eyes are turned, for You are a gracious and merciful God King.

And rebuild Jerusalem the holy city speedily in our days. Be blessed, God, rebuilder — in His mercy — of Jerusalem. Amen

Be blessed, God, our god, King of the universe, the god Who is our Father, our King, our Mighty One, our Creator, our Redeemer, our Maker, our Holy-One, the Holy-One of Jacob, our Shepherd — Israel's Shepherd — the King Who is good and does good to all, Who every day did good, does good, will do good to all of us; Who bestowed, bestows and will bestow favors on us forever: grace, lovingkindness, mercy and relief, succor and prosperity, blessing and salvation, consolation, maintenance and sustenance, and life, and peace, and all that is good; and may He never let us lack for any good thing.

The Merciful — forever may He reign over us. The Merciful — may He be blessed in Heaven and on earth. The Merciful — may He be praised for all generations, and may He glory in us forever and for all time, and take pride in us forever and for all eternity. The Merciful — may He grant us honorable sustenance. The Merciful — may He break the yoke from our neck and may He lead us proud and erect back to our land. The Merciful — may He send ample blessing on this house and on this table at which we have eaten. The Merciful — may He send us Prophet Elijah so fondly remembered, to bring us good tidings, salvations and consolations.

The Merciful — may He bless the State of Israel, the first sprouting of the Final Redemption, and the soldiers of the Israel Defense Forces.

The Merciful — may He bless

(children at their parents' table say) my father and teacher, and my mother my teacher — them and their household and their children and all that is theirs,

(parents at their own table say the appropriate part/s of the following) me, my wife (husband) and my progeny and all that is mine,

וּבְנֵה יְרוּשָׁלַיִם עִיר הַקֹּדֶשׁ בִּמְהֵרָה בְיָמֵינוּ
בָּרוּךְ אַתָּה יְיָ בּוֹנֵה בְרַחֲמָיו יְרוּשָׁלָיִם אָמֵן:

בָּרוּךְ אַתָּה יְיָ אֱלֹהֵינוּ מֶלֶךְ הָעוֹלָם הָאֵל אָבִינוּ
מַלְכֵּנוּ אַדִּירֵנוּ בּוֹרְאֵנוּ גֹּאֲלֵנוּ יוֹצְרֵנוּ קְדוֹשֵׁנוּ
קְדוֹשׁ יַעֲקֹב רוֹעֵנוּ רוֹעֵה יִשְׂרָאֵל הַמֶּלֶךְ הַטּוֹב
וְהַמֵּטִיב לַכֹּל שֶׁבְּכָל יוֹם וָיוֹם הוּא הֵטִיב הוּא
מֵטִיב הוּא יֵיטִיב לָנוּ · הוּא גְמָלָנוּ הוּא גוֹמְלֵנוּ
הוּא יִגְמְלֵנוּ לָעַד לְחֵן לְחֶסֶד וּלְרַחֲמִים וּלְרֶוַח
הַצָּלָה וְהַצְלָחָה בְּרָכָה וִישׁוּעָה נֶחָמָה פַּרְנָסָה
וְכַלְכָּלָה וְרַחֲמִים וְחַיִּים וְשָׁלוֹם וְכָל טוֹב וּמִכָּל
טוּב אַל יְחַסְּרֵנוּ:

הָרַחֲמָן · הוּא יִמְלוֹךְ עָלֵינוּ לְעוֹלָם וָעֶד:
הָרַחֲמָן · הוּא יִתְבָּרַךְ בַּשָּׁמַיִם וּבָאָרֶץ:
הָרַחֲמָן הוּא יִשְׁתַּבַּח לְדוֹר דּוֹרִים וְיִתְפָּאַר בָּנוּ
לָנֶצַח נְצָחִים וְיִתְהַדַּר בָּנוּ לָעַד וּלְעוֹלְמֵי
עוֹלָמִים: הָרַחֲמָן הוּא יְפַרְנְסֵנוּ בְּכָבוֹד: הָרַחֲמָן
הוּא יִשְׁבּוֹר עֻלֵּנוּ מֵעַל צַוָּארֵנוּ וְהוּא יוֹלִיכֵנוּ
קוֹמְמִיּוּת לְאַרְצֵנוּ: הָרַחֲמָן הוּא יִשְׁלַח לָנוּ בְּרָכָה
מְרֻבָּה בַּבַּיִת הַזֶּה וְעַל שֻׁלְחָן זֶה שֶׁאָכַלְנוּ עָלָיו:
הָרַחֲמָן הוּא יִשְׁלַח לָנוּ אֶת אֵלִיָּהוּ הַנָּבִיא זָכוּר
לַטּוֹב וִיבַשֶּׂר לָנוּ בְּשׂוֹרוֹת טוֹבוֹת יְשׁוּעוֹת
וְנֶחָמוֹת: הָרַחֲמָן הוּא יְבָרֵךְ אֶת־אָבִי מוֹרִי בַּעַל
הַבַּיִת הַזֶּה · וְאֶת־אִמִּי מוֹרָתִי בַּעֲלַת הַבַּיִת
הַזֶּה · אוֹתָם וְאֶת בֵּיתָם וְאֶת־זַרְעָם וְאֶת־כָּל־

אֲשֶׁר לָהֶם*אוֹתָנוּ וְאֶת כָּל אֲשֶׁר לָנוּ כְּמוֹ שֶׁנִּתְבָּרְכוּ אֲבוֹתֵינוּ אַבְרָהָם יִצְחָק וְיַעֲקֹב בַּכֹּל מִכֹּל כֹּל כֵּן יְבָרֵךְ אוֹתָנוּ כֻּלָּנוּ יַחַד בִּבְרָכָה שְׁלֵמָה וְנֹאמַר אָמֵן:

בַּמָּרוֹם יְלַמְּדוּ עֲלֵיהֶם וְעָלֵינוּ זְכוּת שֶׁתְּהִי לְמִשְׁמֶרֶת שָׁלוֹם וְנִשָּׂא בְרָכָה מֵאֵת יְיָ וּצְדָקָה מֵאֱלֹהֵי יִשְׁעֵנוּ: וְנִמְצָא־חֵן וְשֵׂכֶל טוֹב בְּעֵינֵי אֱלֹהִים וְאָדָם:

לשבת הָרַחֲמָן הוּא יַנְחִילֵנוּ יוֹם שֶׁכֻּלוֹ שַׁבָּת וּמְנוּחָה לְחַיֵּי הָעוֹלָמִים:

הָרַחֲמָן הוּא יַנְחִילֵנוּ יוֹם שֶׁכֻּלוֹ טוֹב:
הָרַחֲמָן הוּא יְזַכֵּנוּ לִימוֹת הַמָּשִׁיחַ וּלְחַיֵּי הָעוֹלָם הַבָּא: מִגְדִּל יְשׁוּעוֹת מַלְכּוֹ וְעֹשֶׂה חֶסֶד לִמְשִׁיחוֹ לְדָוִד וּלְזַרְעוֹ עַד עוֹלָם. עֹשֶׂה שָׁלוֹם בִּמְרוֹמָיו הוּא יַעֲשֶׂה שָׁלוֹם עָלֵינוּ וְעַל כָּל יִשְׂרָאֵל וְאִמְרוּ אָמֵן:

יְראוּ אֶת יְיָ קְדֹשָׁיו כִּי אֵין מַחְסוֹר לִירֵאָיו כְּפִירִים רָשׁוּ וְרָעֵבוּ וְדֹרְשֵׁי יְיָ לֹא יַחְסְרוּ כָל־טוֹב: הוֹדוּ לַיְיָ כִּי טוֹב כִּי לְעוֹלָם חַסְדּוֹ: פּוֹתֵחַ אֶת יָדֶיךָ וּמַשְׂבִּיעַ לְכָל חַי רָצוֹן: בָּרוּךְ הַגֶּבֶר אֲשֶׁר יִבְטַח בַּיְיָ וְהָיָה יְיָ מִבְטַחוֹ:*

יְיָ עֹז לְעַמּוֹ יִתֵּן יְיָ יְבָרֵךְ אֶת עַמּוֹ בַשָּׁלוֹם:
בָּרוּךְ אַתָּה יְיָ אֱלֹהֵינוּ מֶלֶךְ הָעוֹלָם בּוֹרֵא פְּרִי הַגָּפֶן:

(guests say) the master of this house — him and his wife the mistress of this house, them and their children and all that is theirs,

and all others seated at this table, us and all that is ours. Just as our fathers Abraham, Isaac and Jacob were blessed with all, of all, all, so may He bless us, all of us together, with a perfect blessing; and let us say: Amen.

On High may there be invoked for them and for us such merit as will be a safeguard of peace, and so that we may carry a blessing from God and justice from our Saving-God, and so that we may "win favor and approbation from God and the peoples." (Proverbs 3:4)

(say only on Sabbath)
The Merciful — may He grant us the Day-That-Is-All Sabbath and repose of the Life-That-Is-To-Be.

The Merciful — may He bequeath to us a Day That Is All Good.
The Merciful — may He judge us worthy of the Messianic Era and the life of the World-That-Is-To-Be.
"He Who gives His king great victories, Who deals graciously with His anointed one — with David and his descendants for ever." (Samuel II 22:51)
"He keeps His high spheres in harmony" (Job 25:2) — may He grant harmony to us and to all Israel. Now say: Amen.

"Fear God, you, His holy ones; for those who fear Him want for nothing." (Psalms 34:10) "Lions have been reduced to starvation, those who seek God lack no good thing." (Psalms 34:11) "Give thanks to God, for He is good; for His lovingkindness endures forever." (Psalms 118:1) "You give openhandedly, filling the need of every living creature." (Psalms 145:16) "Blessed is he who trusts in God and rests his confidence in God." (Jeremiah 17:7) "I was a lad and now am old, and never have I seen a righteous person forsaken, his children begging bread." (Psalms 37:35) "May God grant His people strength, may God bless His people with well-being." (Psalms 29:11)

Say the following blessing and drink the third cup, reclining.

Be blessed, God, our God, King of the universe, Creator of the fruit of the vine.

Seder at the Emanuel Residence Club in San Francisco

An annual event in San Francisco was the second seder held at the Emanuel Residence Club for women, on Page Street. The seder began in 1924 and was conducted annually with the participation of the residents and members of the community.

A reporter from KCBS radio broadcast this report on April 8,1955.

"Along with some 200 other guests, I was invited to the Seder at the Emanuel Residence Club out on Page Street.

"This is the historic Feast of the Passover, and with special foods and rituals, we recalled the days of long ago when Moses led the Jewish people from the bondage of Egypt. As the ancient ceremony unfolded, I noticed that some of the guests, who had been to Seders all their lives, were not as attentive to the words of Rabbi Saul White, of Temple Beth Sholom, as I would have thought.

"But then a change came over the celebration as the Rabbi asked Mr. Ben Swig to read an addition to the Seder service that was prepared in honor of the Jews who died in the uprising of the Warsaw ghetto in the past war. And as Mr. Swig recounted the loss of 6 million of his people under Hitler, who made the work of the Pharaohs but child's play in comparison, when he recounted the bravery of those who rose up against the Nazis to defend the honor of the name of Israel, a great change occurred. The ancient ceremony was now modern and meaningful to us. And all participated with a will in the final blessing that prayed for the hastening of the day when swords shall at last be broken, wars ended, and mankind freed from violence, be united in an eternal covenant of brotherhood."

Celebrating Passover at the Emanuel Residence Club in 1920s.
Western Jewish History Center of the Judah L. Magnes Museum, Berkeley, California

Seder Ritual of Remembrance

למען תזכור!
Lest We Forget!

For the six million Jews who perished
at the hands of the Nazis
and for the heroes of the ghetto uprisings

We Remember The Six Million

On this seder night when we review the history of our people, we pause to recall with deep pain the darkest chapter which was written in our own century. Six million innocent Jews — men, women and children — were brutally put to death by the Nazis, far more cruel than any Pharaoh had ever been.

On this night marking the revolt in the Warsaw Ghetto, we remember the resistance of the Jews in Hitler's Europe. Starving, weakened by disease, weighted down by oppression, tormented by the slaughter of their mothers and fathers, their children, their brothers and sisters, they somehow found the strength to rise up against their oppressors.

There are no words to comfort us for this terrible loss. Nor shall we ever be able to forget it. Indeed, we do not want to forget it. For if we do not remember the Six Million, then they die a second time.

When we remember them, they live again in us and through us.

One of the most remarkable stories that has come to us out of those terrible days concerns an old Jewish prayer. The prayer expresses the firm belief that one day a messenger of God will arrive and announce a time of brotherly love and peace among all men. This prayer was set to a moving melody and sung by our condemned Jewish brothers and sisters on their way to death in the gas chambers. They refused to give up the hope that a brighter tomorrow would come. Their hope is a challenge to us, to build that world in which they believed.

The Seder Ritual of Remembrance
was created by Rufus Learsi, a noted writer,
in 1953. It has become a part of many sedarim
in the USA and in other parts of the world.

Fill Elijah's cup, open the front door, and say:

Pour out Thy wrath on the nations that know Thee not and on the kingdoms that do not invoke Thy Name. For they have devoured Jacob and laid waste his homestead. (Psalms 79:6-7) Pour out Thy fury on them and let Thy blazing anger overtake them. (Psalms 69:25) Pursue them in anger and exterminate them from under God's skies. (Lamentations 3:66)

Close the door Fill the fourth cup.

Hallel

Not to us, God, not to us, but to Your Name ascribe the glory for Your lovingkindness, for Your constancy. Why should the nations say: "Where, then, is their God?" — when our God is in heaven, doing whatever He wishes. Their idols are silver and gold, the work of human hands. They have a mouth but speak not; eyes they have but they do not see. They have ears but they do not hear; nose they have but they smell not; hands — but they do not feel; feet — but they do not walk; their throat cannot utter a sound. Their makers become like them, and so do all who trust in them. Israel trusts in God — He is their help and shield. The House of Aaron trusts in God — He is their help and shield. The God-fearers trust in God — He is their help and shield. (Psalms 115:1-11)

God remembers us — He will bless: He will bless the House of Israel. He will bless the House of Aaron. He will bless the God-fearers — the small and the great alike. May God give you increase — you and your children. Blessed are you of God, Maker of the heavens and earth. The heavens are God's heavens, but the earth He gave to Man. Not the dead praise God, not those who go down to the Realm-of-Silence. But we shall bless God, now and forever. Halleluiah (Psalms 115:12-18)

מוזגין כוס שלישי.

שְׁפֹךְ חֲמָתְךָ אֶל הַגּוֹיִם אֲשֶׁר לֹא יְדָעוּךָ וְעַל מַמְלָכוֹת אֲשֶׁר בְּשִׁמְךָ לֹא קָרָאוּ: כִּי אָכַל אֶת יַעֲקֹב וְאֶת נָוֵהוּ הֵשַׁמּוּ: שְׁפָךְ עֲלֵיהֶם זַעְמֶךָ וַחֲרוֹן אַפְּךָ יַשִּׂיגֵם: תִּרְדֹּף בְּאַף וְתַשְׁמִידֵם מִתַּחַת שְׁמֵי יְיָ:

הַלֵּל

מוזגין כוס רביעי.

לֹא לָנוּ יְהֹוָה לֹא לָנוּ כִּי לְשִׁמְךָ תֵּן כָּבוֹד עַל חַסְדְּךָ עַל אֲמִתֶּךָ • לָמָּה יֹאמְרוּ הַגּוֹיִם אַיֵּה נָא אֱלֹהֵיהֶם: וֵאלֹהֵינוּ בַשָּׁמָיִם כֹּל אֲשֶׁר חָפֵץ עָשָׂה: עֲצַבֵּיהֶם כֶּסֶף וְזָהָב מַעֲשֵׂה יְדֵי אָדָם: פֶּה לָהֶם וְלֹא יְדַבֵּרוּ עֵינַיִם לָהֶם וְלֹא יִרְאוּ: אָזְנַיִם לָהֶם וְלֹא יִשְׁמָעוּ אַף לָהֶם וְלֹא יְרִיחוּן: יְדֵיהֶם וְלֹא יְמִישׁוּן רַגְלֵיהֶם וְלֹא יְהַלֵּכוּ לֹא יֶהְגּוּ בִּגְרוֹנָם: כְּמוֹהֶם יִהְיוּ עֹשֵׂיהֶם כֹּל אֲשֶׁר בֹּטֵחַ בָּהֶם: יִשְׂרָאֵל בְּטַח בַּיהֹוָה עֶזְרָם וּמָגִנָּם הוּא: בֵּית אַהֲרֹן בִּטְחוּ בַיהֹוָה עֶזְרָם וּמָגִנָּם הוּא: יִרְאֵי יְהֹוָה בִּטְחוּ בַיהֹוָה עֶזְרָם וּמָגִנָּם הוּא:

יְיָ זְכָרָנוּ יְבָרֵךְ יְבָרֵךְ אֶת בֵּית יִשְׂרָאֵל יְבָרֵךְ אֶת בֵּית אַהֲרֹן: יְבָרֵךְ יִרְאֵי יְיָ הַקְּטַנִּים עִם הַגְּדֹלִים: יֹסֵף יְיָ עֲלֵיכֶם עֲלֵיכֶם וְעַל בְּנֵיכֶם: בְּרוּכִים אַתֶּם לַיָי עֹשֵׂה שָׁמַיִם וָאָרֶץ: הַשָּׁמַיִם שָׁמַיִם לַיָי וְהָאָרֶץ נָתַן לִבְנֵי אָדָם: לֹא הַמֵּתִים יְהַלְלוּ יָהּ וְלֹא כָּל יֹרְדֵי דוּמָה: וַאֲנַחְנוּ נְבָרֵךְ יָהּ מֵעַתָּה וְעַד עוֹלָם הַלְלוּיָהּ:

אָהַבְתִּי כִּי יִשְׁמַע יְיָ אֶת קוֹלִי תַּחֲנוּנָי: כִּי הִטָּה אָזְנוֹ
לִי וּבְיָמַי אֶקְרָא : אֲפָפוּנִי חֶבְלֵי מָוֶת וּמְצָרֵי שְׁאוֹל
מְצָאוּנִי צָרָה וְיָגוֹן אֶמְצָא : וּבְשֵׁם יְיָ אֶקְרָא אָנָּה יְיָ
מַלְּטָה נַפְשִׁי : חַנּוּן יְיָ וְצַדִּיק וֵאלֹהֵינוּ מְרַחֵם : שֹׁמֵר
פְּתָאיִם יְיָ דַּלּוֹתִי וְלִי יְהוֹשִׁיעַ : שׁוּבִי נַפְשִׁי לִמְנוּחָיְכִי כִּי יְיָ
גָּמַל עָלָיְכִי : כִּי חִלַּצְתָּ נַפְשִׁי מִמָּוֶת אֶת עֵינִי מִן דִּמְעָה
אֶת רַגְלִי מִדֶּחִי : אֶתְהַלֵּךְ לִפְנֵי יְיָ בְּאַרְצוֹת הַחַיִּים :
הֶאֱמַנְתִּי כִּי אֲדַבֵּר אֲנִי עָנִיתִי מְאֹד : אֲנִי אָמַרְתִּי בְחָפְזִי
כָּל הָאָדָם כֹּזֵב :

מָה אָשִׁיב לַיְיָ כָּל תַּגְמוּלוֹהִי עָלָי : כּוֹס
יְשׁוּעוֹת אֶשָּׂא וּבְשֵׁם יְיָ אֶקְרָא : נְדָרַי לַיְיָ
אֲשַׁלֵּם נֶגְדָה נָּא לְכָל עַמּוֹ : יָקָר בְּעֵינֵי יְיָ
הַמָּוְתָה לַחֲסִידָיו : אָנָּה יְיָ כִּי אֲנִי עַבְדֶּךָ אֲנִי
עַבְדְּךָ בֶּן אֲמָתֶךָ פִּתַּחְתָּ לְמוֹסֵרָי : לְךָ אֶזְבַּח
זֶבַח תּוֹדָה וּבְשֵׁם יְיָ אֶקְרָא : נְדָרַי לַיְיָ אֲשַׁלֵּם
נֶגְדָה נָּא לְכָל עַמּוֹ : בְּחַצְרוֹת בֵּית יְיָ בְּתוֹכֵכִי
יְרוּשָׁלָיִם הַלְלוּיָהּ :

הַלְלוּ אֶת יְיָ כָּל גּוֹיִם שַׁבְּחוּהוּ כָּל הָאֻמִּים :
כִּי גָבַר עָלֵינוּ חַסְדּוֹ וֶאֱמֶת יְיָ לְעוֹלָם הַלְלוּיָהּ :

ק'הודו   הוֹדוּ לַיְיָ כִּי טוֹב   כִּי לְעוֹלָם חַסְדּוֹ : ק'הודו
ק'הודו   יֹאמַר נָא יִשְׂרָאֵל   כִּי לְעוֹלָם חַסְדּוֹ : ק'הודו
ק'הודו   יֹאמְרוּ נָא בֵית אַהֲרֹן   כִּי לְעוֹלָם חַסְדּוֹ : ק'הודו
ק'הודו   יֹאמְרוּ נָא יִרְאֵי יְיָ   כִּי לְעוֹלָם חַסְדּוֹ : ק'הודו

I yearn that God should hear my supplicating voice, that He should bend His ear to me whenever in my lifetime I cry out. The coils of death are taking me in their grip, the torments of Hell are overtaking me, trouble and anguish are my lot. So I call out in God's Name: "Please, God, save my life!" Gracious is God, and just; our god is merciful, God protects the simple; when I am down and out He will save me. Rest again, my soul, for God has been good to you. For You have rescued me from death, my eyes from weeping, my feet from stumbling. I will walk in God's presence in the realm of the living. I trusted (in God) even when I thought I was finished, when I was at my wit's end, when in my desperation I said: "All people are untrustworthy."
(Psalms 116:1-11)

How can I repay God for all His bounties to me? I will raise the cup of salvation and invoke God's name. I will pay my vows to God in the presence of all His people. Grievous in God's eyes is the death of His faithful ones. Please, God — I am indeed Your servant; I am Your servant, son of Your maidservant; You have loosed my bonds. To You I will bring a Thanks-offering, and I will invoke God's name. I will pay my vows to God in the presence of His entire people. In the courts of God's House in the heart of Jerusalem. Halleluiah.
(Psalms 116:12-19)

Praise God, all you nations; laud Him, all peoples. For great is His lovingkindness towards us, and God's constancy is everlasting. Halleluiah. (Psalms 117)

Give thanks to God, for He is good   *For His grace endures forever.*
Say it now, Israel   *For His grace endures forever.*
Say it now, House of Aaron   *For His grace endures forever.*
Say it now, God-fearers   *For His grace endures forever.*

(Psalms 118:1-4)

U.S. Congressional
Hearing on Mailing of Matzoh

MAILING OF MATZOH

HEARING
BEFORE THE
SUBCOMMITTEE ON
POSTAL FACILITIES AND MAIL
OF THE
COMMITTEE ON
POST OFFICE AND CIVIL SERVICE
HOUSE OF REPRESENTATIVES
NINETY-SECOND CONGRESS
SECOND SESSION

APRIL 12, 1972

Serial No. 92–39

Printed for the use of the
Committee on Post Office and Civil Service

U.S. GOVERNMENT PRINTING OFFICE
77-961 O   WASHINGTON : 1972

Cover of the proceedings of the "Hearing on Mailing of Matzoh" held during the 92nd Congress

Mail hope to 3,000,000 Jews in the Soviet Union

CLIP THIS MAILING LABEL!

On March 17, 1972, use it to mail a one-pound box of matzoh to the Soviet Ambassador in Washington.

The thousands of boxes will serve as your testimony of opposition to the tyranny of imprisonment of 3-million Jews in the Soviet Union.

CLIP HERE

This matzoh, the symbol of freedom for 3,200 years, now symbolizes hope for 3-million Jews of the Soviet Union, and reminds you that freedom-loving Americans stand with them in their struggle.

PLACE 65¢ POSTAGE HERE

FREE THE PRISONERS—LET MY PEOPLE GO

FROM:

FRAGILE

POSTMASTER:
PARCEL POST

TO:
Ambassador Anatoly Dobrynin
EMBASSY OF THE U.S.S.R.
1706 18th Street N.W.
Washington, D.C. 20009

A PROJECT OF THE N.J. REGIONAL ADVISORY BOARD, ANTI-DEFAMATION LEAGUE OF B'NAI B'RITH

These labels were distributed throughout New Jersey and Pennsylvania to encourage participation in the campaign.

MAILING OF MATZOH

WEDNESDAY, APRIL 12, 1972

U.S. HOUSE OF REPRESENTATIVES

The subcommittee on Postal Facilities and Mail met pursuant to notice, at 10:30 a.m., room 219 of the Cannon House Office Building, the Honorable Robert N.C. Nix, presiding.

Today, we will take testimony on an incident involving the mailing of unleavened bread during the Passover season to the Russian Embassy for Jews in the Soviet Union, who are not allowed to produce their own matzoh for the holy season.

These mailings were the result of a campaign by interested American citizens to dramatize the plight of Jews behind the Iron Curtain. The Embassy refused to accept these mailings. The amount of material mailed amounted to 8,000 pounds and over 4,000 individual mailings.

The Postal Service kept this material approximately a week; and then destroyed it. B'nai B'rith, an honorable and highly respected organization, offered to take the material from the Postal Service for distribution to the poor rather than see it destroyed.

Matzoh has a religious and historical significance to the Jewish people. Its destruction, during the Passover season, has created a serious and vital question as to whether or not the Postal Service should have disposed of this food to organizations ready to supply it to the needy in the face of requests from such organizations.

This is taken from the first page of the proceedings and explains why the hearing was conducted.

Matzah Pardon

Matzah served as a route to freedom for a prisoner who requested unleavened bread and a Haggadah from Rabbi Tobias Geffen of Atlanta, Georgia. Arrested in 1932 and sentenced to the Georgia Chain Gang after innocently hitching a ride with bank robbers, he did not hesitate to seek the supplies needed to observe Passover. His letter of April 1933 set into motion a chain of events resulting in the Governor of Georgia, Eugene Talmadge, "granting clemency" to the prisoner.

Rabbi T. Geffen

Atlanta, Georgia

Prison Farm
Milledgeville, Ga.
April 22, 1933

Dear Rabbi:

Please excuse me for my tardiness in answering your letter. I have just been released from solitary confinement due to my refusal to work during Passover.

And just as our people of old received the manna from the heavens, just so did I receive the package of Passover food you so kindly sent me.

Indeed to me, it was as though it came from the heavens. The Warden here brought it to me in the cell in which I was confined. This was done on his own initiative as the Prision Commission's rules doesn't call for such an act.

And some day I pray to God I may be in position to thank you in a more befitting way than in a mere letter.

So again thanking you with all my heart and hoping that I may see you to do so personally soon.

I am very gratefully yours

November 6, 1933

Hon. Eugene Talmadge
Governor State of Georgia
Executive Department
Atlanta, Georgia

Honored Sir:

About six months ago, during the Passover Holidays the prisoner wrote to me from the State Farm and requested that I send him a Passover Prayer Book and also the special Passover food. From this I can readily understand that the boy has a deep religious feeling and also possesses character, sufficient to warrant my recommendation that he be granted clemency.

Very sincerely yours,

Rabbi Tobias Geffen

Executive Department
Atlanta

Eugene Talmadge
Governor

Tom Linder
Secretary Executive Department

November 3, 1933

Rabbi Tobias Geffen
593 Washington Street, S. W.,
Atlanta, Georgia.

Dear Rabbi Geffen:
The case of the prisoner was presented to me this morning on a petition for clemency.
I have been informed that you are interested in this matter and recommend that I grant clemency for this applicant.

Sincerely yours,
Eugene Talmadge

In my distress I called on God; He answered by setting me free. God is with me; I have no fear: What can people do to me? God is with me helping me, so I shall gloat over my enemies. It is better to trust in God than to trust in people. It is better to trust in God than to trust in the great. All the nations have beset me; but in God's Name I will surely rout them. They surround me on all sides; but in God's Name I will surely rout them. They surround me like bees at the honeycomb; they attack me like flames at the stubble; but in God's Name I will surely rout them. They wanted to knock me down, but God helped me. God is my strength and my power, and He has become my salvation. Joyous shouts of deliverance resound in the tents of the righteous: God's right hand is triumphant. I shall not die — I shall live, and proclaim God's works. God chastened me severely, but He did not hand me over to death. Open the gates of victory to me: I would enter them, I would give thanks to God. This is God's gate — the victors enter through it. (Psalms 118:5-20)

I thank You for You have answered me, and You have become my salvation. (Repeat) The stone that the builders rejected has become the chief cornerstone. (Repeat) This is God's doing: it is marvelous in our eyes. (Repeat) This is the day on which God acted: let us exult and rejoice on it. (Repeat) (Psalms 118:21-24)

Please, God, deliver us! (Repeat)

Please, God, let us prosper! (Repeat) (Psalms 118:25)

מִן־הַמֵּצַר קָרָאתִי יָּהּ עָנָנִי בַמֶּרְחָב יָהּ: יְיָ לִי לֹא אִירָא מַה־יַּעֲשֶׂה לִי אָדָם: יְיָ לִי בְּעֹזְרָי וַאֲנִי אֶרְאֶה בְשֹׂנְאָי: טוֹב לַחֲסוֹת בַּיְיָ מִבְּטֹחַ בָּאָדָם: טוֹב לַחֲסוֹת בַּיְיָ מִבְּטֹחַ בִּנְדִיבִים: כָּל־גּוֹיִם סְבָבוּנִי בְּשֵׁם יְיָ כִּי אֲמִילַם: סַבּוּנִי גַם־סְבָבוּנִי בְּשֵׁם יְיָ כִּי אֲמִילַם: סַבּוּנִי כִדְבֹרִים דֹּעֲכוּ כְּאֵשׁ קוֹצִים בְּשֵׁם יְיָ כִּי אֲמִילַם: דָּחֹה דְחִיתַנִי לִנְפֹּל וַיְיָ עֲזָרָנִי: עָזִּי וְזִמְרָת יָהּ וַיְהִי־לִי לִישׁוּעָה: קוֹל רִנָּה וִישׁוּעָה בְּאָהֳלֵי צַדִּיקִים יְמִין יְיָ עֹשָׂה חָיִל: יְמִין יְיָ רוֹמֵמָה יְמִין יְיָ עֹשָׂה חָיִל: לֹא־אָמוּת כִּי־אֶחְיֶה וַאֲסַפֵּר מַעֲשֵׂי יָהּ: יַסֹּר יִסְּרַנִּי יָּהּ וְלַמָּוֶת לֹא נְתָנָנִי: פִּתְחוּ־לִי שַׁעֲרֵי־צֶדֶק אָבֹא בָם אוֹדֶה יָהּ: זֶה־הַשַּׁעַר לַיְיָ צַדִּיקִים יָבֹאוּ בוֹ:

אוֹדְךָ   אוֹדְךָ כִּי עֲנִיתָנִי וַתְּהִי־לִי לִישׁוּעָה:

אֶבֶן   אֶבֶן מָאֲסוּ הַבּוֹנִים הָיְתָה לְרֹאשׁ פִּנָּה:

מֵאֵת   מֵאֵת יְיָ הָיְתָה זֹּאת הִיא נִפְלָאת בְּעֵינֵינוּ:

זֶה   זֶה הַיּוֹם עָשָׂה יְיָ נָגִילָה וְנִשְׂמְחָה בוֹ:

אָנָּא יְיָ הוֹשִׁיעָה נָּא   אָנָּא יְיָ הוֹשִׁיעָה נָּא
אָנָּא יְיָ הַצְלִיחָה נָּא   אָנָּא יְיָ הַצְלִיחָה נָּא:

בָּרוּךְ   בָּרוּךְ הַבָּא בְּשֵׁם יְיָ בֵּרַכְנוּכֶם מִבֵּית יְיָ:

יְיָ   אֵל יְיָ וַיָּאֶר לָנוּ אִסְרוּ־חַג בַּעֲבֹתִים עַד קַרְנוֹת הַמִּזְבֵּחַ:

אֵלִי אַתָּה וְאוֹדֶךָּ אֱלֹהַי אֲרוֹמְמֶךָּ:

הוֹדוּ   הוֹדוּ לַיְיָ כִּי־טוֹב כִּי לְעוֹלָם חַסְדּוֹ:

May all who enter be blessed in God's Name; we bless you from God's House. (Repeat) God is God, and He has given us light; bind the Festival Offering with branches to the altar's horns. (Repeat) You are my God and I will thank You, my God — and I will extol You. (Repeat) Give thanks to God, for He is good; His grace endures forever. (Repeat)   (Psalms 118:126-129)

כִּי לְעוֹלָם חַסְדּוֹ:	קלו הוֹדוּ לַיהוָה כִּי־טוֹב	Give thanks to God, for He is good;
		His grace endures forever.
כִּי לְעוֹלָם חַסְדּוֹ:	הוֹדוּ לֵאלֹהֵי הָאֱלֹהִים	Give thanks to Lord-of-all-the-Lords;
		His grace endures forever.
כִּי לְעוֹלָם חַסְדּוֹ:	הוֹדוּ לַאֲדֹנֵי הָאֲדֹנִים	Give thanks to God-of-all-the-gods,
		His grace endures forever.
כִּי לְעוֹלָם חַסְדּוֹ:	לְעֹשֵׂה נִפְלָאוֹת גְּדֹלוֹת לְבַדּוֹ	To Him Who alone works great marvels;
		His grace endures forever.
כִּי לְעוֹלָם חַסְדּוֹ:	לְעֹשֵׂה הַשָּׁמַיִם בִּתְבוּנָה	To Him Who made the heavens with
		wisdom; *His grace endures forever.*
כִּי לְעוֹלָם חַסְדּוֹ:	לְרֹקַע הָאָרֶץ עַל־הַמָּיִם	To Him Who laid the earth on the waters;
		His grace endures forever.
כִּי לְעוֹלָם חַסְדּוֹ:	לְעֹשֵׂה אוֹרִים גְּדֹלִים	To Him Who made great lights;
		His grace endures forever.
כִּי לְעוֹלָם חַסְדּוֹ:	אֶת־הַשֶּׁמֶשׁ לְמֶמְשֶׁלֶת בַּיּוֹם	The sun to rule by day;
		His grace endures forever.
כ"לח":	אֶת־הַיָּרֵחַ וְכוֹכָבִים לְמֶמְשְׁלוֹת בַּלָּיְלָה	The moon and stars to rule by night;
		His grace endures forever.
כִּי לְעוֹלָם חַסְדּוֹ:	לְמַכֵּה מִצְרַיִם בִּבְכוֹרֵיהֶם	To Him Who struck Egypt through their
		firstborn; *His grace endures forever.*
כִּי לְעוֹלָם חַסְדּוֹ:	וַיּוֹצֵא יִשְׂרָאֵל מִתּוֹכָם	And brought Israel out of their midst;
		His grace endures forever.
כִּי לְעוֹלָם חַסְדּוֹ:	בְּיָד חֲזָקָה וּבִזְרוֹעַ נְטוּיָה	With strong hand and an outstretched arm;
		His grace endures forever.
כִּי לְעוֹלָם חַסְדּוֹ:	לְגֹזֵר יַם־סוּף לִגְזָרִים	To Him Who split apart the Reed Sea;
		His grace endures forever.
כִּי לְעוֹלָם חַסְדּוֹ:	וְהֶעֱבִיר יִשְׂרָאֵל בְּתוֹכוֹ	And led Israel right through it;
		His grace endures forever.
כִּי לְעוֹלָם חַסְדּוֹ:	וְנִעֵר פַּרְעֹה וְחֵילוֹ בְיַם־סוּף	But hurled Pharaoh and his host into the
		Reed Sea; *His grace endures forever.*
כִּי לְעוֹלָם חַסְדּוֹ:	לְמוֹלִיךְ עַמּוֹ בַּמִּדְבָּר	To Him Who led His people through the
		wilderness; *His grace endures forever.*
כִּי לְעוֹלָם חַסְדּוֹ:	לְמַכֵּה מְלָכִים גְּדֹלִים	To Him Who struck down mighty kings;
		His grace endures forever.
כִּי לְעוֹלָם חַסְדּוֹ:	וַיַּהֲרֹג מְלָכִים אַדִּירִים	And also slew great potentates ;
		His grace endures forever.
כִּי לְעוֹלָם חַסְדּוֹ:	לְסִיחוֹן מֶלֶךְ הָאֱמֹרִי	Sihon King of the Amorites;
		His grace endures forever.
כִּי לְעוֹלָם חַסְדּוֹ:	וּלְעוֹג מֶלֶךְ הַבָּשָׁן	And Og King of Bashan;
		His grace endures forever.
כִּי לְעוֹלָם חַסְדּוֹ:	וְנָתַן אַרְצָם לְנַחֲלָה	And then He bequeathed their land;
		His grace endures forever.
כִּי לְעוֹלָם חַסְדּוֹ:	נַחֲלָה לְיִשְׂרָאֵל עַבְדּוֹ	To His servant Israel to have;
		His grace endures forever.
כִּי לְעוֹלָם חַסְדּוֹ:	שֶׁבְּשִׁפְלֵנוּ זָכַר־לָנוּ	Who remembered us when we were down
		and out; *His grace endures forever.*
כִּי לְעוֹלָם חַסְדּוֹ:	וַיִּפְרְקֵנוּ מִצָּרֵינוּ	And rescued us from our enemies;
		His grace endures forever.
כִּי לְעוֹלָם חַסְדּוֹ:	נֹתֵן לֶחֶם לְכָל־בָּשָׂר	Who supplies food to all flesh;
		His grace endures forever.
כִּי לְעוֹלָם חַסְדּוֹ:	הוֹדוּ לְאֵל הַשָּׁמָיִם	Thank the God-of-all-Heavens;
		His grace endures forever.

(Psalms 136)

The Reed Sea Split into Twelve Channels

Through the centuries, the crossing of the Reed Sea has been illustrated by Jewish and Christian artists alike. An 1851 Haggadah issued by L.H. Frank of New York was the first American version to depict the splitting of the sea.

The signed drawing below appears in the Liberman-Chicago Haggadah and is the first illustration of this crucial event in the Exodus saga by an American artist, H. Senior. In his "modern" portrayal, the artist shows twelve "channels" in the sea, one for each of the twelve tribes. A pillar of fire leads them as Moses stands behind urging the Israelites to hurry and escape the pursuing Egyptians.

Haggadah for Passover ed. Hayyim Liberman, Chicago, 1879

נִשְׁמַת כָּל חַי תְּבָרֵךְ אֶת שִׁמְךָ יְיָ אֱלֹהֵינוּ. וְרוּחַ כָּל
בָּשָׂר תְּפָאֵר וּתְרוֹמֵם זִכְרְךָ מַלְכֵּנוּ תָּמִיד. מִן הָעוֹלָם
וְעַד הָעוֹלָם אַתָּה אֵל. וּמִבַּלְעָדֶיךָ אֵין לָנוּ מֶלֶךְ גּוֹאֵל
וּמוֹשִׁיעַ פּוֹדֶה וּמַצִּיל וּמְפַרְנֵס וּמְרַחֵם בְּכָל עֵת צָרָה
וְצוּקָה אֵין לָנוּ מֶלֶךְ אֶלָּא אַתָּה: אֱלֹהֵי הָרִאשׁוֹנִים
וְהָאַחֲרוֹנִים. אֱלוֹהַּ כָּל בְּרִיּוֹת אֲדוֹן כָּל תּוֹלָדוֹת הַמְהֻלָּל
בְּרֹב הַתִּשְׁבָּחוֹת הַמְנַהֵג עוֹלָמוֹ בְּחֶסֶד וּבְרִיּוֹתָיו
בְּרַחֲמִים. וַיְיָ לֹא יָנוּם וְלֹא יִישָׁן. הַמְעוֹרֵר יְשֵׁנִים
וְהַמֵּקִיץ נִרְדָּמִים. וְהַמֵּשִׂיחַ אִלְּמִים. וְהַמַּתִּיר אֲסוּרִים
וְהַסּוֹמֵךְ נוֹפְלִים וְהַזּוֹקֵף כְּפוּפִים. לְךָ לְבַדְּךָ אֲנַחְנוּ
מוֹדִים. אִלּוּ פִינוּ מָלֵא שִׁירָה כַּיָּם וּלְשׁוֹנֵנוּ רִנָּה כַּהֲמוֹן
גַּלָּיו וְשִׂפְתוֹתֵינוּ שֶׁבַח כְּמֶרְחֲבֵי רָקִיעַ. וְעֵינֵינוּ מְאִירוֹת
כַּשֶּׁמֶשׁ וְכַיָּרֵחַ. וְיָדֵינוּ פְרוּשׂוֹת כְּנִשְׁרֵי שָׁמָיִם. וְרַגְלֵינוּ
קַלּוֹת כָּאַיָּלוֹת: אֵין אֲנַחְנוּ מַסְפִּיקִים לְהוֹדוֹת לְךָ יְיָ
אֱלֹהֵינוּ וֵאלֹהֵי אֲבוֹתֵינוּ. וּלְבָרֵךְ אֶת שִׁמְךָ. עַל אַחַת
מֵאָלֶף אֶלֶף אַלְפֵי אֲלָפִים וְרִבֵּי רְבָבוֹת פְּעָמִים הַטּוֹבוֹת
שֶׁעָשִׂיתָ עִם אֲבוֹתֵינוּ וְעִמָּנוּ: מִמִּצְרַיִם גְּאַלְתָּנוּ יְיָ אֱלֹהֵינוּ
וּמִבֵּית עֲבָדִים פְּדִיתָנוּ בְּרָעָב זַנְתָּנוּ וּבְשָׂבָע כִּלְכַּלְתָּנוּ.

The breath of every living thing blesses Your Name, God, our God, and the spirit of all flesh glorifies and extols the memory of You, our King, always. Since ever forever God You are, and besides You we have no king who liberates and saves, redeeming, rescuing, providing and exercising mercy in every time of trouble and distress. We have no king but You. God of first and last, God of all creatures, Lord of all the born, Who is lauded with manifold praises, Who directs His universe with lovingkindness and His creatures with mercy. And God does not slumber or sleep — He Who awakens the sleeping and rouses the slumbering, and gives speech to the muted and sets free the imprisoned and supports the falling and straightens the bent — to You alone we give thanks. Even if our mouth were an ocean of song, and our tongue were rolling seas of exultation, our lips spacious skies of praise, our eyes radiant as the sun and the moon, our hands outspread like soaring eagles, and our feet as fleet as the hinds — with all this we would still not be able to thank You, God, our God and God of our fathers, and to bless Your Name for even one-thousandth-of-a-thousandth-of-a-thousandth-of-a-ten-thousandth of a myriad of all the favors You granted our ancestors and us. From Egypt You liberated us, God, our God, from slavery You emancipated us. In famine You fed us,

Jewish Welfare Board
Passover greeting card
Philip Goodman Collection

providing plentifully. From the swords You saved us and from pestilence rescued us, from terrible, deadly diseases You delivered us. Till now Your mercies have succored us, Your lovingkindness has not failed us. So, God, do not ever fail us. Therefore, the limbs that You have shaped in us, and the breath and spirit that You have breathed into our nostrils, and the tongue that You have placed in our mouth — they, all of them, shall give thanks and bless and praise and glorify and exalt and revere and hallow and enthrone Your Name, our King. Indeed, every mouth shall acknowledge You, every tongue shall swear allegiance to You, every knee shall bend to You, every erect body shall prostrate itself before You, all hearts shall fear You, all innards shall sing to Your Name,

מֵחֶרֶב הִצַּלְתָּנוּ. וּמִדֶּבֶר מִלַּטְתָּנוּ וּמֵחֳלָיִם רָעִים וְנֶאֱמָנִים דִּלִּיתָנוּ: עַד הֵנָּה עֲזָרוּנוּ רַחֲמֶיךָ. וְלֹא עֲזָבוּנוּ חֲסָדֶיךָ. וְאַל תִּטְּשֵׁנוּ יְיָ אֱלֹהֵינוּ לָנֶצַח: עַל כֵּן אֵבָרִים שֶׁפִּלַּגְתָּ בָּנוּ. וְרוּחַ וּנְשָׁמָה שֶׁנָּפַחְתָּ בְּאַפֵּינוּ וְלָשׁוֹן אֲשֶׁר שַׂמְתָּ בְּפִינוּ: הֵן הֵם יוֹדוּ וִיבָרְכוּ וִישַׁבְּחוּ וִיפָאֲרוּ וִירוֹמְמוּ וְיַעֲרִיצוּ וְיַקְדִּישׁוּ וְיַמְלִיכוּ אֶת שִׁמְךָ מַלְכֵּנוּ: כִּי כָל פֶּה לְךָ יוֹדֶה. וְכָל לָשׁוֹן לְךָ תִשָּׁבַע. וְכָל בֶּרֶךְ לְךָ תִכְרַע. וְכָל קוֹמָה לְפָנֶיךָ תִשְׁתַּחֲוֶה. וְכָל לְבָבוֹת יִירָאוּךָ. וְכָל קֶרֶב וּכְלָיוֹת יְזַמְּרוּ לִשְׁמֶךָ. כַּדָּבָר שֶׁכָּתוּב כָּל עַצְמוֹתַי תֹּאמַרְנָה יְיָ מִי כָמוֹךָ. מַצִּיל עָנִי מֵחָזָק מִמֶּנּוּ וְעָנִי וְאֶבְיוֹן מִגֹּזְלוֹ: מִי יִדְמֶה לָּךְ וּמִי יִשְׁוֶה לָּךְ וּמִי יַעֲרָךְ לָךְ. הָאֵל הַגָּדוֹל הַגִּבּוֹר וְהַנּוֹרָא אֵל עֶלְיוֹן קוֹנֵה שָׁמַיִם וָאָרֶץ: נְהַלֶּלְךָ וּנְשַׁבֵּחֲךָ וּנְפָאֶרְךָ וּנְבָרֵךְ אֶת שֵׁם קָדְשֶׁךָ. כָּאָמוּר לְדָוִד בָּרְכִי נַפְשִׁי אֶת יְיָ וְכָל קְרָבַי אֶת שֵׁם קָדְשׁוֹ: הָאֵל בְּתַעֲצֻמוֹת עֻזֶּךָ הַגָּדוֹל בִּכְבוֹד שְׁמֶךָ: הַגִּבּוֹר לָנֶצַח וְהַנּוֹרָא בְּנוֹרְאוֹתֶיךָ: הַמֶּלֶךְ הַיּוֹשֵׁב עַל כִּסֵּא רָם וְנִשָּׂא:

as written, "All my bones shall say, 'God, who is like You — rescuing the wretched from those stronger than them, the poor and the needy from their despoilers'!" (Psalms 35:10) Who is like You, who can be compared to You, who can equal You — the Great, Mighty and Awesome God, the Supreme God, Creator-of-Heaven-and-Earth?! We shall praise You, laud You, glorify You, and bless Your holy Name, as said, "Bless God, O my soul; all my being — bless His holy Name!" (Psalms 103:1) God in the vastness of Your power, great in the glory of Your Name, mighty forever, and awesome in Your awe-inspiring acts, King enthroned in a high and exalted seat —

The sale of matzah each year was an opportunity to generate funds for Jewish communal and educational institutions. The matzah campaign was an annual event in Buffalo, New York, from 1931-1939.

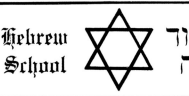

שׁוֹכֵן עַד מָרוֹם וְקָדוֹשׁ שְׁמוֹ. וְכָתוּב רַנְּנוּ צַדִּיקִים בַּיי לַיְשָׁרִים נָאוָה תְהִלָּה: בְּפִי יְשָׁרִים תִּתְהַלָּל. וּבְדִבְרֵי צַדִּיקִים תִּתְבָּרַךְ. וּבִלְשׁוֹן חֲסִידִים תִּתְרוֹמָם. וּבְקֶרֶב קְדוֹשִׁים תִּתְקַדָּשׁ. וּבְמַקְהֲלוֹת רִבְבוֹת עַמְּךָ בֵּית יִשְׂרָאֵל בְּרִנָּה יִתְפָּאֵר שִׁמְךָ מַלְכֵּנוּ בְּכָל־דּוֹר וָדוֹר שֶׁכֵּן חוֹבַת כָּל־הַיְצוּרִים לְפָנֶיךָ יְיָ אֱלֹהֵינוּ וֵאלֹהֵי אֲבוֹתֵינוּ לְהוֹדוֹת לְהַלֵּל לְשַׁבֵּחַ לְפָאֵר לְרוֹמֵם לְהַדֵּר לְבָרֵךְ לְעַלֵּה וּלְקַלֵּס עַל כָּל־דִּבְרֵי שִׁירוֹת וְתִשְׁבְּחוֹת דָּוִד בֶּן־יִשַׁי עַבְדְּךָ מְשִׁיחֶךָ: יִשְׁתַּבַּח שִׁמְךָ לָעַד מַלְכֵּנוּ הָאֵל הַמֶּלֶךְ הַגָּדוֹל וְהַקָּדוֹשׁ בַּשָּׁמַיִם וּבָאָרֶץ כִּי לְךָ נָאֶה יְיָ אֱלֹהֵינוּ וֵאלֹהֵי אֲבוֹתֵינוּ שִׁיר וּשְׁבָחָה הַלֵּל וְזִמְרָה עֹז וּמֶמְשָׁלָה נֶצַח גְּדֻלָּה וּגְבוּרָה תְּהִלָּה וְתִפְאֶרֶת קְדֻשָּׁה וּמַלְכוּת בְּרָכוֹת וְהוֹדָאוֹת מֵעַתָּה וְעַד עוֹלָם: בָּרוּךְ אַתָּה יְיָ אֵל מֶלֶךְ גָּדוֹל בַּתִּשְׁבָּחוֹת אֵל הַהוֹדָאוֹת אֲדוֹן הַנִּפְלָאוֹת הַבּוֹחֵר בְּשִׁירֵי זִמְרָה מֶלֶךְ אֵל חֵי הָעוֹלָמִים:

Inhabiter-of-Eternity-in-a-High-and-Holy-Place is His name. And it is written, "Exult in God, O you righteous; it befits the upright to acclaim Him." (Psalms 33:1) By the mouth of the upright You shall be praised, and by the lips of the righteous You shall be blessed, and by the tongues of the pious You shall be exalted, and by the innards of the holy You shall be hallowed.

And in the assemblies of the myriads of Your people the House of Israel shall Your Name, O our king, be glorified in joyous song in every generation. For it is the duty of all creatures, God, our god and god of our fathers, to give thanks, to praise, laud, glorify, extol, honor, bless, exalt and adore You even beyond all the songs and praises of David son of Jesse Your servant, Your anointed one.

Forever praised is Your Name, our king — God, great and holy King in heaven and on earth. Because You are worthy — God, our God and God of our fathers — of song and laudation, praise and psalmody, power and dominion, victory, greatness and might, fame and glory, sanctity and sovereignty, blessings and thanksgiving to Your great and holy Name, for You are God, now and forever. Be blessed, God, God, King, sublime in praises, God for thanksgiving, Lord of wonders, Who prefers songs of psalmody, Sole King, God, Ever-living One.

As the Passover cuisine expanded in the USA, dairy products assumed a broader role in the holiday diet. The Raskas Dairy company of St. Louis, founded in 1888, developed a variety of Kosher for Passover products including Smetina, sweet butter, whipped butter and cream cheese.

Raskas Company Archives, St. Louis, Missouri

All Your works shall praise You, God, our god and Your Devotees — the righteous who do Your will — and Your entire people the House of Israel shall exultantly give thanks, bless, laud, glorify, exalt, adore, hallow, and declare the kingship of Your Name, our king. For it is good to thank You, and it is fitting to sing Your Name, because now and forever You are God. Be blessed, God — King extolled by paeans of praise.

Lift the cup of wine, say the following blessing, and drink the fourth cup, reclining.

Be blessed, God, King of the universe, Creator of the fruit of the vine.

Say the concluding Blessing-after-Wine

Be blessed, God, our god, King of the universe, for the vine and the fruit of the vine, and for the yield of the field, and for the land so lovely, so good and so spacious that You saw fit to bequeath to our ancestors to eat of its produce and sate ourselves on its bounty. Have mercy, God, our god, on Israel Your people and on Jerusalem Your city and on Zion the abode of Your glory, on Your altar and on Your shrine. Rebuild Jerusalem the holy city speedily in our days. And bring us back up to it and let us rejoice in its upbuilding, let us eat of its fruit and sate ourselves on its bounty and we will

יְהַלְלוּךָ יְיָ אֱלֹהֵינוּ עַל כָּל מַעֲשֶׂיךָ· וַחֲסִידֶיךָ צַדִּיקִים עוֹשֵׂי רְצוֹנֶךָ וְכָל עַמְּךָ בֵּית יִשְׂרָאֵל בְּרִנָּה יוֹדוּ וִיבָרְכוּ וִישַׁבְּחוּ וִיפָאֲרוּ וִירוֹמְמוּ וְיַעֲרִיצוּ וְיַקְדִּישׁוּ וְיַמְלִיכוּ אֶת שִׁמְךָ מַלְכֵּנוּ כִּי לְךָ טוֹב לְהוֹדוֹת וּלְשִׁמְךָ נָאֶה לְזַמֵּר כִּי מֵעוֹלָם וְעַד עוֹלָם אַתָּה אֵל:

בָּרוּךְ אַתָּה יְיָ אֱלֹהֵינוּ מֶלֶךְ הָעוֹלָם בּוֹרֵא פְּרִי הַגָּפֶן:

בָּרוּךְ אַתָּה יְיָ אֱלֹהֵינוּ מֶלֶךְ הָעוֹלָם עַל הַגֶּפֶן וְעַל פְּרִי הַגֶּפֶן וְעַל תְּנוּבַת הַשָּׂדֶה וְעַל אֶרֶץ חֶמְדָּה טוֹבָה וּרְחָבָה שֶׁרָצִיתָ וְהִנְחַלְתָּ לַאֲבוֹתֵינוּ לֶאֱכוֹל מִפִּרְיָהּ וְלִשְׂבּוֹעַ מִטּוּבָהּ רַחֵם (נָא) יְיָ אֱלֹהֵינוּ עַל יִשְׂרָאֵל עַמֶּךָ וְעַל יְרוּשָׁלַיִם עִירֶךָ וְעַל צִיּוֹן מִשְׁכַּן כְּבוֹדֶךָ וְעַל מִזְבְּחֶךָ וְעַל הֵיכָלֶךָ וּבְנֵה יְרוּשָׁלַיִם עִיר הַקֹּדֶשׁ בִּמְהֵרָה בְיָמֵינוּ וְהַעֲלֵנוּ לְתוֹכָהּ. וְשַׂמְּחֵנוּ בְּבִנְיָנָהּ. וְנֹאכַל מִפִּרְיָהּ וְנִשְׂבַּע מִטּוּבָהּ וּנְבָרֶכְךָ עָלֶיהָ בִּקְדֻשָּׁה וּבְטָהֳרָה: *בשבת* וּרְצֵה וְהַחֲלִיצֵנוּ בְּיוֹם הַשַּׁבָּת הַזֶּה·* כִּי אַתָּה יְיָ טוֹב וּמֵטִיב לַכֹּל וְנוֹדֶה לְךָ עַל הָאָרֶץ וְעַל פְּרִי הַגָּפֶן. בָּרוּךְ אַתָּה יְיָ עַל הָאָרֶץ וְעַל פְּרִי הַגָּפֶן:

bless You for it in holiness and purity. (On Sabbath say: And may it please You to strengthen us on this Sabbath day) And grant us joy on this Matzot Festival Day, for You, God, are good and You do good to all. We thank You for the Land and for the fruit of its vine. Be blessed, God, for the Land and for the fruit of its vine.

Gershom Mendes Seixas (1746-1816), the Hazzan of the Shearith Israel Synagogue in New York, was an American patriot who did not wish to live under British rule. He was able to flee with his family in 1776 just before the British captured the city and eventually served as the Hazzan of Mikve Israel in Philadelphia during the latter part of the Revolutionary War. With the war over, his New York congregation expected him to return and resume his duties.

Missing the Family on Passover

March 15th, 1784
Philadelphia, Pa.

Mr. Hayman Levy
President
Shearith Israel Congregation

Dear & Worthy Sir

Should the Prayer of the Letter (that I can stay in Philadelphia until the new month of Iyar) not be thought Eligible you will please let me know by Post - & I'll be with you for Shabbat Hagadol - & leave my Family till after Pesah - tho' - you must allow it to be a great Hardship for a Man to be without His Family on a Pesah.

Gershom Mendes Seixas

If you will it, it is no legend *Theodor Herzl*

To an American Zionist who was here a year ago it is a thrilling experience to be in Israel this Passover and especially to be in Jerusalem. I remember vividly the meeting of the Actions Committee in Tel Aviv just before Passover a year ago. Jerusalem was cut off. The arrival of a few of our colleagues from Jerusalem to join the meeting of the Actions Committee was a stirring event. They were greeted by their colleagues in Tel Aviv as if they came from

Dr. Israel Goldstein (1896-1986) and Mrs. Bert Goldstein (1895-) made aliyah to Jerusalem, Israel in 1960.

the other end of the world. The whole of Palestine was a battlefield and Jerusalem was at the very heart of Israel's battle for survival.

At that meeting and under those circumstances the decision was reached to proclaim the Jewish State and the proclamation was then drafted. It was an act of faith, as great as any in Jewish history, as great an act of faith as that which led Israel of old to plunge into the Red Sea in quest of the Promised Land. There was no turning back then and there was no turning back a year ago. And this act of faith has been vindicated by a victory as great and as miraculous as the "yeziat mizrayim," "the exodus from Egypt," and "keriat yam suf," "splitting of the Red Sea." I think I am also able to convey to you the thoughts and the feelings of Jews in America. I am sure they will read the Haggadah this Passover in the light of the great events of the first year, that they will be thinking of their brothers and sisters in Israel with pride and thanksgiving, and that when they finish the Seder Service with the exclamation, "leshana haba'a beyerushalayim," "next year in Jerusalem," many thousands of American Jews will mean those words literally not figuratively. They will plan to be here with you next Passover. Perhaps hundreds if not thousands will plan to remain and to settle here.

It has been a wonderful year for Jerusalem and for Israel. For all the deliverance from political oppression and from physical peril, for all the emergence out of darkness into light, and for all the heroic resistance and the final victory, in which men and women, young and old, have played their part, we lift the Passover cup and we say, "Hallelujah!"

Passover Radio Message, Dr. Israel Goldstein, April 11, 1949

My love for Zion was kindled in 1904 when I was nine. Sitting on the porch with my Grandpa one evening in July, I noticed tears in his eyes and asked him what was wrong. He told me that Theodor Herzl had just died, and he explained Herzl's dream of a Jewish state. "Bert, he said one day you will live to see the Jewish state reborn."

Jerusalem today is a wondrous city. Never does a day pass when I do not learn something new about the city or hear about an innovative devlopment. My blessing for Jerusalem is that it may grow and be a precious gem crowning the land of Israel, the homeland of the Jewish people.

Bert Goldstein

נִרְצָה כי כבר רצה האלהים את מעשיך.

חֲסַל סִדּוּר פֶּסַח כְּהִלְכָתוֹ. כְּכָל מִשְׁפָּטוֹ וְחֻקָּתוֹ.
כַּאֲשֶׁר זָכִינוּ לְסַדֵּר אוֹתוֹ. כֵּן נִזְכֶּה לַעֲשׂוֹתוֹ: זָךְ שׁוֹכֵן
מְעוֹנָה. קוֹמֵם קְהַל מִי מָנָה: קָרֵב נַהֵל נִטְעֵי כַנָּה.
פְּדוּיִם לְצִיּוֹן בְּרִנָּה:

לְשָׁנָה הַבָּאָה בִּירוּשָׁלָיִם:

Nirtza

We've made another Seder just as we were told.
We followed all the rules laid down in days of old.
Just as we've been privileged to do it now with care,
May God grant us the chance to do it every year.

Pure-One, O, You pure Dweller-of-the-Realm-Above:
Restore Your countless people,
   bring them home with love;
Quickly take Your vine shoots and
   replant them strong
Back in Zion's vineyard,
   where they will sing your song.

Next year in
Jerusalem-Rebuilt!

It Happened at Midnight

בְּלֵיל רִאשׁוֹנָה אוֹמְרִים זֶה:

וּבְכֵן וַיְהִי בַּחֲצִי הַלַּיְלָה:

אָז רֹב נִסִּים הִפְלֵאתָ בְּלַיְלָה:
בְּרֹאשׁ אַשְׁמוֹרֶת זֶה הַלַּיְלָה:
גֵּר צֶדֶק נִצַּחְתּוֹ כְּנֶחֱלַק לוֹ לַיְלָה:
וַיְהִי בַּחֲצִי הַלַּיְלָה:

דַּנְתָּ מֶלֶךְ גְּרָר בַּחֲלוֹם הַלַּיְלָה:
הִפְחַדְתָּ אֲרַמִּי בְּאֶמֶשׁ לַיְלָה:
וַיָּשַׂר יִשְׂרָאֵל לְאֵל וַיּוּכַל לוֹ לַיְלָה:
וַיְהִי בַּחֲצִי הַלַּיְלָה:

זֶרַע בְּכוֹרֵי פַתְרוֹס מָחַצְתָּ בַּחֲצִי הַלַּיְלָה:
חֵילָם לֹא מָצְאוּ בְּקוּמָם בַּלַּיְלָה:
טִסַּת נְגִיד חֲרֹשֶׁת סִלִּיתָ בְּכוֹכְבֵי לַיְלָה:
וַיְהִי בַּחֲצִי הַלַּיְלָה:

יָעַץ מְחָרֵף לְנוֹפֵף אִוּוּי הוֹבַשְׁתָּ פְגָרָיו בַּלַּיְלָה:
כָּרַע בֵּל וּמַצָּבוֹ בְּאִישׁוֹן לַיְלָה:
לְאִישׁ חֲמוּדוֹת נִגְלָה רָז חֲזוֹת לַיְלָה:
וַיְהִי בַּחֲצִי הַלַּיְלָה:

In times of yore You wrought most miracles at night,
In the early watches of this night;
You granted Abraham victory at night.
It happened at midnight.

Gerar's king You judged in a dream by night;
You startled Laban in the dark of night;
Jacob fought and bested an angel by night.
It happened at midnight.

Egypt's firstborn You smote at midnight;
They could not find their wealth when they rose at night;
Sisera You routed through stars of the night;
It happened at midnight.

Sennacherib's legions You devastated by night;
Babylon's god was overthrown in the dark of night;
Daniel was shown the secret of Your mysteries of the night;
It happened at midnight.

Passover Seders

Conducted By
JAN PEERCE

DEAUVILLE HOTEL
NAPOLEON ROOM

First Seder — April 2, 1969
7:00 P.M.

Second Seder — April 3, 1969
7:00 P.M.

Menu

Traditional Bitter Herbs   Sacramental Wine
Charoses, Hard Boiled Egg, Salt Water
Crisp Celery Hearts   Rosebud Radishes
Stuffed Fresh Water Fish, Beet Horseradish
Chicken Broth with Matzoh Ball
ROAST HALF SPRING CHICKEN
Deauville Dressing
Potato Kugel   Carrot Tzimmes
Tossed Green Salad
French Dressing
Honey Cake
Lemon Sponge Cake   Passover Macaroons
Cafe Noir   Orange Pekoe Tea

Well-known Jewish musicians often appeared at a hotel seder. Jan Peerce (1904-1984), a Metropolitan Opera star and noted artist, conducted the sedarim at the Deauville Hotel in Miami Beach, Florida in 1969.

82

Drunken Belshazzar was killed
this very night;
Daniel was saved from the lions'
den at night;
Haman wrote evil decrees in the
night;
It happened at midnight.

You arose and vanquished him by
Ahasuerus's sleepless night;
You will help those who ask:
"What of the night?"
You will call: "Morning follows
the night."
It happened at midnight.

Speed the day that is neither day
nor night;
Most High, proclaim that Yours is
the day and also the night;
Set guards over Your city all day
and all night;
Make bright as day the darkness
of the night;
May it all happen at midnight.

מִשְׁתַּכֵּר בִּכְלֵי קֹדֶשׁ נֶהֱרַג בּוֹ בַּלַּיְלָה:
נוֹשַׁע מִבּוֹר אֲרָיוֹת פּוֹתֵר בִּעֲתוּתֵי לַיְלָה:
שִׂנְאָה נָטַר אֲגָגִי וְכָתַב סְפָרִים בַּלַּיְלָה:
וַיְהִי בַּחֲצִי הַלַּיְלָה:

עוֹרַרְתָּ נִצְחֲךָ עָלָיו בְּנֶדֶד שְׁנַת לַיְלָה:
תִּדְרוֹךְ לְשׁוֹמֵר מַה מִּלַּיְלָה:
צָרַח כַּשּׁוֹמֵר וְשָׂח אָתָא בֹקֶר וְגַם לַיְלָה:
וַיְהִי בַּחֲצִי הַלַּיְלָה:

קָרֵב יוֹם אֲשֶׁר הוּא לֹא יוֹם וְלֹא לַיְלָה:
רָם הוֹדַע כִּי לְךָ הַיּוֹם אַף לְךָ הַלַּיְלָה:
שׁוֹמְרִים הַפְקֵד לְעִירְךָ כָּל הַיּוֹם וְכָל הַלַּיְלָה:
תָּאִיר כְּאוֹר יוֹם חֶשְׁכַת לַיְלָה:
וַיְהִי בַּחֲצִי הַלַּיְלָה:

This V-Mail Passover Greeting was prepared
by Chaplain Ralph Ben-Zion (Weisberger)
for the personnel at his post. While
stationed in the Persian Gulf in April, 1944,
he sent one to his sister.

Ralph M. Ben-Zion (Weisberger) Collection

וּבְכֵן, וַאֲמַרְתֶּם זֶבַח פֶּסַח:

אֹמֶץ גְּבוּרוֹתֶיךָ הִפְלֵאתָ   בַּפֶּסַח:

בְּרֹאשׁ כָּל מוֹעֲדוֹת נִשֵּׂאתָ   פֶּסַח:

גִּלִּיתָ לְאֶזְרָחִי חֲצוֹת לֵיל   פֶּסַח:

וַאֲמַרְתֶּם זֶבַח פֶּסַח:

דְּלָתָיו דָּפַקְתָּ כְּחֹם הַיּוֹם   בַּפֶּסַח:

הִסְעִיד נוֹצְצִים עֻגוֹת מַצּוֹת   בַּפֶּסַח:

וְאֶל הַבָּקָר רָץ זֵכֶר לְשׁוֹר עֵרֶךְ   פֶּסַח:

וַאֲמַרְתֶּם זֶבַח פֶּסַח:

זֹעֲמוּ סְדוֹמִים וְלֹהֲטוּ בָּאֵשׁ   פֶּסַח:

חֻלַּץ לוֹט מֵהֶם וּמַצּוֹת אָפָה בְּקֵץ   פֶּסַח:

טֵאטֵאתָ אַדְמַת מֹף וְנֹף בְּעָבְרְךָ   בַּפֶּסַח:

וַאֲמַרְתֶּם זֶבַח פֶּסַח:

יָהּ רֹאשׁ כָּל אוֹן מָחַצְתָּ בְּלֵיל שִׁמּוּר   פֶּסַח:

כַּבִּיר עַל בֵּן בְּכוֹר פָּסַחְתָּ בְּדַם   פֶּסַח:

לְבִלְתִּי תֵּת מַשְׁחִית לָבֹא בִּפְתָחַי   בַּפֶּסַח:

וַאֲמַרְתֶּם זֶבַח פֶּסַח:

```
■■■■■■■■■■■■■■■■■■■■■■■■■■■■■■■■■■■■■■■

            ADMIT ONE
        Pesach Entertainment
               Given by
    SHEARITH ISRAEL SUNDAY SCHOOL
   AT THE CONGREGATION SHEARITH ISRAEL
        ───────────────
   SUNDAY, APRIL 17th, 1932—6:30 P. M.
        ───────────────
         ADMISSION 15 CENTS

■■■■■■■■■■■■■■■■■■■■■■■■■■■■■■■■■■■■■■■
```

Congregational Hebrew schools and Talmud Torahs utilized Passover as an opportunity for community events. At this congregation in Atlanta, Georgia, in 1932, a play was given by the students to an appreciative audience and then a magician mystified the crowd.

On the second night:
Thus you will say:
this is the Passover Offering

Your wondrous powers You displayed on Passover;
Above all festivals You set Passover;
You revealed Yourself to Abraham at midnight of Passover.
And you shall say:
This is the Passover Offering.

At Abraham's door You knocked at high noon on Passover;
He fed the angels matzot on Passover;
To the cattle he ran for the ox on Passover;
And you shall say:
This is the Passover Offering.

The Sodomites enraged God and were burned on Passover;
Lot was saved, and he baked matzot on Passover;
You swept Egypt as You passed through on Passover;
And you shall say:
This is the Passover Offering.

God, You crushed the firstborn on Passover night;
But Your own firstborn You spared by the sign of the blood
The Destroyer did not enter our homes on Passover;
And you shall say:
This is the Passover Offering.

Jericho was taken on Passover;
Gideon felled Midian through a
barley-cake dream on Passover;
Assyria's legions were consumed on
Passover.

And you shall say:
This is the Passover Offering.

Sennacherib halted to shun the siege
on Passover;
A hand wrote Babylon's doom on
the wall on Passover;
Feasting Babylon was conquered on
Passover.

And you shall say:
This is the Passover Offering.

Esther assembled the people for a
three-day fast on Passover;
You crushed Haman on a gallows
tree on Passover;
You will punish Edom doubly on
Passover;
Let Your might free us as it did then
on the night of Passover;

And you shall say:
This is the Passover Offering.

מִסְגֶּרֶת סֻגָּרָה בְּעִתּוֹתֵי פֶּסַח:
נִשְׁמְדָה מִדְיָן בִּצְלִיל שְׂעוֹרֵי עֹמֶר פֶּסַח:
שֹׂרְפוּ מִשְׁמַנֵּי פוּל וְלוּד בִּיקַר יְקוֹד פֶּסַח:
וַאֲמַרְתֶּם זֶבַח פֶּסַח:

עוֹד הַיּוֹם בְּנֹב לַעֲמוֹד עַד גָּעָה עוֹנַת פֶּסַח:
פַּס יָד כָּתְבָה לְקַעֲקֵעַ צוּל בַּפֶּסַח:
צָפֹה הַצָּפִית עָרוֹךְ הַשֻּׁלְחָן בַּפֶּסַח:
וַאֲמַרְתֶּם זֶבַח פֶּסַח:

קָהָל כִּנְּסָה הֲדַסָּה לְשַׁלֵּשׁ צוֹם בַּפֶּסַח:
רֹאשׁ מִבֵּית רָשָׁע מָחַצְתָּ בְּעֵץ חֲמִשִּׁים בַּפֶּסַח:
שְׁתֵּי אֵלֶּה רֶגַע תָּבִיא לְעוּצִית בַּפֶּסַח:
תָּעֹז יָדְךָ תָּרוּם יְמִינְךָ כְּלֵיל הִתְקַדֶּשׁ חַג פֶּסַח:
וַאֲמַרְתֶּם זֶבַח פֶּסַח:

Holiday Appearance in the Gold Country

Feast of Passover — In commemoration of
the beginning of Passover, the Hebrew
fellow citizens closed their places of
business last Monday evening. Tuesday was
observed by old and young, male and
female. Although not so strictly observed,
the remainder of the week wore a holiday
appearance. The Passover will end next
Tuesday evening.

Sonora Union Democrat April 11, 1868,
Sonora, California. This reference cited in
Robert E. Levinson, *The Jews in the
California Gold Rush*, Berkeley, 1978, p.116.
Sonora, California in the early 1860s

כִּי לוֹ נָאֶה ● כִּי לוֹ יָאֶה:

אַדִּיר בִּמְלוּכָה. בָּחוּר כַּהֲלָכָה. גְּדוּדָיו יֹאמְרוּ לוֹ.
לְךָ וּלְךָ. לְךָ כִּי לְךָ. לְךָ אַף לְךָ. לְךָ יְיָ הַמַּמְלָכָה:
כִּי לוֹ נָאֶה. כִּי לוֹ יָאֶה: דָּגוּל בִּמְלוּכָה. הָדוּר כַּהֲלָכָה.
וָתִיקָיו יֹאמְרוּ לוֹ. לְךָ וּלְךָ. לְךָ כִּי לְךָ. לְךָ אַף לְךָ
לְךָ יְיָ הַמַּמְלָכָה: כִּי לוֹ נָאֶה. כִּי לוֹ יָאֶה: זַכַּי
בִּמְלוּכָה. חָסִין כַּהֲלָכָה. טַפְסְרָיו יֹאמְרוּ לוֹ. לְךָ וּלְךָ. לְךָ
כִּי לְךָ. לְךָ אַף לְךָ. לְךָ יְיָ הַמַּמְלָכָה: כִּי לוֹ נָאֶה. כִּי לוֹ
יָאֶה: יָחִיד בִּמְלוּכָה. כַּבִּיר כַּהֲלָכָה. לִמּוּדָיו יֹאמְרוּ לוֹ.
לְךָ וּלְךָ. לְךָ כִּי לְךָ. לְךָ אַף לְךָ. לְךָ יְיָ הַמַּמְלָכָה: כִּי
לוֹ נָאֶה. כִּי לוֹ יָאֶה: מָרוֹם בִּמְלוּכָה. נוֹרָא כַּהֲלָכָה.
סְבִיבָיו יֹאמְרוּ לוֹ. לְךָ וּלְךָ. לְךָ כִּי לְךָ. לְךָ אַף לְךָ. לְךָ
יְיָ הַמַּמְלָכָה: כִּי לוֹ נָאֶה. כִּי לוֹ יָאֶה: עָנָיו בִּמְלוּכָה.
פּוֹדֶה כַּהֲלָכָה. צַדִּיקָיו יֹאמְרוּ לוֹ. לְךָ וּלְךָ. לְךָ כִּי לְךָ.
לְךָ אַף לְךָ. לְךָ יְיָ הַמַּמְלָכָה: כִּי לוֹ נָאֶה. כִּי לוֹ יָאֶה:
קָדוֹשׁ בִּמְלוּכָה. רַחוּם כַּהֲלָכָה. שִׁנְאַנָּיו יֹאמְרוּ לוֹ. לְךָ
וּלְךָ. לְךָ כִּי לְךָ. לְךָ אַף לְךָ. לְךָ יְיָ הַמַּמְלָכָה: כִּי לוֹ
נָאֶה. כִּי לוֹ יָאֶה: תַּקִּיף בִּמְלוּכָה. תּוֹמֵךְ כַּהֲלָכָה. תְּמִימָיו
יֹאמְרוּ לוֹ. לְךָ וּלְךָ. לְךָ כִּי לְךָ. לְךָ אַף לְךָ. לְךָ יְיָ
הַמַּמְלָכָה: כִּי לוֹ נָאֶה. כִּי לוֹ יָאֶה:

Ki Lo Naeh

August in kingship, rightfully chosen,
His angel-legions say to Him: "Yours, only Yours, Yours alone,
O Lord, is the kingship!"
It is fitting to praise Him.

Pre-eminent in kingship, truly resplendent,
His faithful say to Him: "Yours, only Yours, Yours alone,
O Lord, is the kingship!"
It is fitting to praise Him.

Pristine in kingship, truly powerful,
His officers say to Him: "Yours, only Yours, Yours alone,
O Lord, is the kingship!"
It is fitting to praise Him.

Unique in kingship, truly mighty,
His disciples say to Him: "Yours, only Yours, Yours alone,
O Lord, is the kingship!"
It is fitting to praise Him.

Exalted in kingship, truly awe-inspiring,
His Heavenly courtiers say to Him: "Yours, only Yours, Yours alone,
O Lord, is the kingship!"
It is fitting to praise Him.

Humble in kingship, truly liberating,
His upright say to Him: "Yours, only Yours, Yours alone,
O Lord, is the kingship!"
It is fitting to praise Him.

Holy in kingship, truly merciful,
His angels say to Him: "Yours, only Yours, Yours alone,
O Lord, is the kingship!"
It is fitting to praise Him.

Mightily sovereign, truly sustaining,
His faultless ones say to Him: "Yours, only Yours, Yours alone,
O Lord, is the kingship!"
It is fitting to praise Him.

August is He -
May He rebuild His Temple very
soon, in our time:
*O God, build; O God, rebuild Your
Temple soon.*

Chosen is He, great is He,
pre-eminent is He;
May He rebuild His Temple very
soon, in our time:
*O God, build; O God, rebuild Your
Temple soon.*

Magnificent is He, venerable is He,
pristine is He;
May He rebuild His Temple very
soon, in our time:
*O God, build; O God, rebuild Your
Temple soon.*

Benevolent is He, pure is He,
one-alone is He;
May He rebuild His Temple very
soon, in our time:
*O God, build; O God, rebuild Your
Temple soon.*

Mighty is He, wise is He, king is He;
May He rebuild His Temple very soon, in our time:
O God, build; O God, rebuild Your Temple soon.

Awesome is He, exalted is He, powerful is He;
May He rebuild His temple very soon, in our time:
O God, build; O God, rebuild Your Temple soon.

Redeemer is He, just is He, holy is he;
May He rebuild His Temple very soon, in our time:
O God, build; O God, rebuild Your Temple soon.

Merciful is He, Almighty is He, potent is He;
May He rebuild His Temple very soon, in our time:
O God, build; O God, rebuild Your Temple soon.

אַדִּיר הוּא יִבְנֶה בֵיתוֹ בְּקָרוֹב, בִּמְהֵרָה, בִּמְהֵרָה, בְּיָמֵינוּ בְּקָרוֹב, אֵל בְּנֵה אֵל בְּנֵה, בְּנֵה בֵיתְךָ בְּקָרוֹב: בָּחוּר הוּא, יִבְנֶה בֵיתוֹ בְּקָרוֹב, בִּמְהֵרָה, בִּמְהֵרָה, בְּיָמֵינוּ בְּקָרוֹב, אֵל בְּנֵה, אֵל בְּנֵה, בְּנֵה בֵיתְךָ בְּקָרוֹב: גָּדוֹל הוּא, דָּגוּל הוּא, יִבְנֶה בֵיתוֹ בְּקָרוֹב, בִּמְהֵרָה, בִּמְהֵרָה, בְּיָמֵינוּ בְּקָרוֹב, אֵל בְּנֵה אֵל בְּנֵה בְּנֵה בֵיתְךָ בְּקָרוֹב: הָדוּר הוּא, וָתִיק הוּא, זַכַּי הוּא חָסִיד הוּא יִבְנֶה בֵיתוֹ בְּקָרוֹב, בִּמְהֵרָה, בִּמְהֵרָה, בְּיָמֵינוּ בְּקָרוֹב, אֵל בְּנֵה, אֵל בְּנֵה, בְּנֵה בֵיתְךָ בְּקָרוֹב: טָהוֹר הוּא, יָחִיד הוּא, כַּבִּיר הוּא לָמוּד הוּא, מֶלֶךְ הוּא, נָאוֹר הוּא, סַגִּיב הוּא, עִזּוּז הוּא, פּוֹדֶה הוּא, צַדִּיק הוּא, יִבְנֶה בֵיתוֹ בְּקָרוֹב, בִּמְהֵרָה, בִּמְהֵרָה, בְּיָמֵינוּ בְּקָרוֹב, אֵל בְּנֵה, אֵל בְּנֵה, בְּנֵה בֵיתְךָ בְּקָרוֹב: קָדוֹשׁ הוּא רַחוּם הוּא, שַׁדַּי הוּא, תַּקִּיף הוּא, יִבְנֶה בֵיתוֹ בְּקָרוֹב, בִּמְהֵרָה, בִּמְהֵרָה, בְּיָמֵינוּ בְּקָרוֹב, אֵל בְּנֵה, אֵל בְּנֵה, בְּנֵה בֵיתְךָ בְּקָרוֹב:

אֶחָד מִי יוֹדֵעַ אֶחָד אֲנִי יוֹדֵעַ. אֶחָד אֱלֹהֵינוּ שֶׁבַּשָּׁמַיִם
וּבָאָרֶץ:

שְׁנַיִם מִי יוֹדֵעַ. שְׁנַיִם אֲנִי יוֹדֵעַ. שְׁנֵי לֻחוֹת הַבְּרִית.
אֶחָד אֱלֹהֵינוּ שֶׁבַּשָּׁמַיִם וּבָאָרֶץ:

שְׁלֹשָׁה מִי יוֹדֵעַ. שְׁלֹשָׁה אֲנִי יוֹדֵעַ. שְׁלֹשָׁה אָבוֹת.
שְׁנֵי לֻחוֹת הַבְּרִית. אֶחָד אֱלֹהֵינוּ שֶׁבַּשָּׁמַיִם וּבָאָרֶץ:

אַרְבַּע מִי יוֹדֵעַ. אַרְבַּע אֲנִי יוֹדֵעַ. אַרְבַּע אִמָּהוֹת,
שְׁלֹשָׁה אָבוֹת. שְׁנֵי לֻחוֹת הַבְּרִית. אֶחָד אֱלֹהֵינוּ
שֶׁבַּשָּׁמַיִם וּבָאָרֶץ:

חֲמִשָּׁה מִי יוֹדֵעַ. חֲמִשָּׁה אֲנִי יוֹדֵעַ. חֲמִשָּׁה חֻמְשֵׁי
תוֹרָה. אַרְבַּע אִמָּהוֹת. שְׁלֹשָׁה אָבוֹת. שְׁנֵי לֻחוֹת
הַבְּרִית. אֶחָד אֱלֹהֵינוּ שֶׁבַּשָּׁמַיִם וּבָאָרֶץ:

שִׁשָּׁה מִי יוֹדֵעַ. שִׁשָּׁה אֲנִי יוֹדֵעַ. שִׁשָּׁה סִדְרֵי מִשְׁנָה.
חֲמִשָּׁה חֻמְשֵׁי תוֹרָה. אַרְבַּע אִמָּהוֹת. שְׁלֹשָׁה אָבוֹת.
שְׁנֵי לֻחוֹת הַבְּרִית. אֶחָד אֱלֹהֵינוּ שֶׁבַּשָּׁמַיִם וּבָאָרֶץ:

שִׁבְעָה מִי יוֹדֵעַ. שִׁבְעָה אֲנִי יוֹדֵעַ. שִׁבְעָה יְמֵי
שַׁבַּתָּא. שִׁשָּׁה סִדְרֵי מִשְׁנָה. חֲמִשָּׁה חֻמְשֵׁי תוֹרָה.
אַרְבַּע אִמָּהוֹת. שְׁלֹשָׁה אָבוֹת. שְׁנֵי לֻחוֹת הַבְּרִית.
אֶחָד אֱלֹהֵינוּ שֶׁבַּשָּׁמַיִם וּבָאָרֶץ:

שְׁמוֹנָה מִי יוֹדֵעַ. שְׁמוֹנָה אֲנִי יוֹדֵעַ. שְׁמוֹנָה יְמֵי
מִילָה. שִׁבְעָה יְמֵי שַׁבַּתָּא. שִׁשָּׁה סִדְרֵי מִשְׁנָה. חֲמִשָּׁה
חֻמְשֵׁי תוֹרָה. אַרְבַּע אִמָּהוֹת. שְׁלֹשָׁה אָבוֹת. שְׁנֵי
לֻחוֹת הַבְּרִית. אֶחָד אֱלֹהֵינוּ שֶׁבַּשָּׁמַיִם וּבָאָרֶץ:

Who Knows One?

Who knows one? I know one!
One is our God in heaven and on earth.

Who knows two? I know two!
Two are the Tablets of the Covenant;
One is our God in heaven and on earth.

Who knows three? I know three!
Three are the Patriarchs,
Two are the Tablets of the Covenant;
One is our God in heaven and on earth.

Who knows four? I know four!
Four are the Matriarchs,
Three are the Patriarchs,
Two are the Tablets of the Covenant;
One is our God in heaven and on earth.

Who knows five? I know five!
Five are the books of the Torah;
Four are the Matriarchs,
Three are the Patriarchs,
Two are the Tablets of the Covenant;
One is our God in heaven and on earth.

Who knows six? I know six!
Six are the orders of the Mishnah;
Five are the books of the Torah;
Four are the Matriarchs,
Three are the Patriarchs,
Two are the Tablets of the Covenant;
One is our God in heaven and on earth.

Who knows seven? I know seven!
Seven are the days of the week;
Six are the orders of the Mishnah;
Five are the books of the Torah;
Four are the Matriarchs,
Three are the Patriarchs,
Two are the Tablets of the Covenant;
One is our God in heaven and on earth.

Who knows eight? I know eight!
Eight are the days to circumcision;
Seven are the days of the week;
Six are the orders of the Mishnah;
Five are the books of the Torah;
Four are the Matriarchs,
Three are the Patriarchs,
Two are the Tablets of the Covenant;
One is our God in heaven and on earth.

Who knows nine? I know nine!
Nine are the months to childbirth;
Eight are the days to circumcision;
Seven are the days of the week;
Six are the orders of the Mishnah;
Five are the books of the Torah;
Four are the Matriarchs,
Three are the Patriarchs,
Two are the Tablets of the Covenant;
One is our God in heaven and on earth.

Who knows ten? I know ten!
Ten are the Commandments of Sinai;
Nine are the months to childbirth;
Eight are the days to circumcision;
Seven are the days of the week;
Six are the orders of the Mishnah;
Five are the books of the Torah;
Four are the Matriarchs,
Three are the Patriarchs,
Two are the Tablets of the Covenant;
One is our God in heaven and on earth.

Who knows eleven? I know eleven!
Eleven are the stars in Joseph's dream;
Ten are the Commandments of Sinai;
Nine are the months to childbirth;
Eight are the days to circumcision;
Seven are the days of the week;
Six are the orders of the Mishnah;
Five are the books of the Torah;
Four are the Matriarchs,
Three are the Patriarchs,
Two are the Tablets of the Covenant;
One is our God in heaven and on earth.

Who knows twelve? I know twelve!
Twelve are the Tribes of Israel;
Eleven are the stars in Joseph's dream;
Ten are the Commandments of Sinai;
Nine are the months to childbirth;
Eight are the days to circumcision;
Seven are the days of the week;
Six are the orders of the Mishnah;
Five are the books of the Torah;
Four are the Matriarchs,
Three are the Patriarchs,
Two are the Tablets of the Covenant;
One is our God in heaven and on earth.

Who knows thirteen? I know thirteen!
Thirteen are God's attributes; Twelve are the Tribes of Israel; Eleven are the stars in Joseph's dream; Ten are the Commandments of Sinai; Nine are the months to childbirth; Eight are the days to circumcision; Seven are the days of the week; Six are the orders of the Mishnah; Five are the books of the Torah; Four are the Matriarchs, Three are the Patriarchs, Two are the Tablets of the Covenant; *One is our God in heaven and on earth.*

תִּשְׁעָה מִי יוֹדֵעַ. תִּשְׁעָה אֲנִי יוֹדֵעַ. תִּשְׁעָה יַרְחֵי לֵידָה. שְׁמוֹנָה יְמֵי מִילָה. שִׁבְעָה יְמֵי שַׁבַּתָּא. שִׁשָּׁה סִדְרֵי מִשְׁנָה. חֲמִשָּׁה חֻמְשֵׁי תוֹרָה. אַרְבַּע אִמָּהוֹת. שְׁלֹשָׁה אָבוֹת. שְׁנֵי לֻחוֹת הַבְּרִית. אֶחָד אֱלֹהֵינוּ שֶׁבַּשָּׁמַיִם וּבָאָרֶץ:

עֲשָׂרָה מִי יוֹדֵעַ. עֲשָׂרָה אֲנִי יוֹדֵעַ. עֲשָׂרָה דִבְּרַיָא. תִּשְׁעָה יַרְחֵי לֵידָה. שְׁמוֹנָה יְמֵי מִילָה. שִׁבְעָה יְמֵי שַׁבַּתָּא. שִׁשָּׁה סִדְרֵי מִשְׁנָה. חֲמִשָּׁה חֻמְשֵׁי תוֹרָה. אַרְבַּע אִמָּהוֹת. שְׁלֹשָׁה אָבוֹת. שְׁנֵי לֻחוֹת הַבְּרִית אֶחָד אֱלֹהֵינוּ שֶׁבַּשָּׁמַיִם וּבָאָרֶץ:

אַחַד עָשָׂר מִי יוֹדֵעַ. אַחַד עָשָׂר אֲנִי יוֹדֵעַ. אַחַד עָשָׂר כּוֹכְבַיָא. עֲשָׂרָה דִבְּרַיָא. תִּשְׁעָה יַרְחֵי לֵידָה. שְׁמוֹנָה יְמֵי מִילָה. שִׁבְעָה יְמֵי שַׁבַּתָּא. שִׁשָּׁה סִדְרֵי מִשְׁנָה. חֲמִשָּׁה חֻמְשֵׁי תוֹרָה. אַרְבַּע אִמָּהוֹת. שְׁלֹשָׁה אָבוֹת שְׁנֵי לֻחוֹת הַבְּרִית. אֶחָד אֱלֹהֵינוּ שֶׁבַּשָּׁמַיִם וּבָאָרֶץ:

שְׁנֵים עָשָׂר מִי יוֹדֵעַ. שְׁנֵים עָשָׂר אֲנִי יוֹדֵעַ. שְׁנֵים עָשָׂר שִׁבְטַיָא. אַחַד עָשָׂר כּוֹכְבַיָא. עֲשָׂרָה דִבְּרַיָא. תִּשְׁעָה יַרְחֵי לֵידָה. שְׁמוֹנָה יְמֵי מִילָה. שִׁבְעָה יְמֵי שַׁבַּתָּא. שִׁשָּׁה סִדְרֵי מִשְׁנָה. חֲמִשָּׁה חֻמְשֵׁי תוֹרָה. אַרְבַּע אִמָּהוֹת. שְׁלֹשָׁה אָבוֹת. שְׁנֵי לֻחוֹת הַבְּרִית. אֶחָד אֱלֹהֵינוּ שֶׁבַּשָּׁמַיִם וּבָאָרֶץ:

שְׁלֹשָׁה עָשָׂר מִי יוֹדֵעַ. שְׁלֹשָׁה עָשָׂר אֲנִי יוֹדֵעַ. שְׁלֹשָׁה עָשָׂר מִדַּיָא. שְׁנֵים עָשָׂר שִׁבְטַיָא. אַחַד עָשָׂר כּוֹכְבַיָא. עֲשָׂרָה דִבְּרַיָא. תִּשְׁעָה יַרְחֵי לֵידָה. שְׁמוֹנָה יְמֵי מִילָה. שִׁבְעָה יְמֵי שַׁבַּתָּא. שִׁשָּׁה סִדְרֵי מִשְׁנָה. חֲמִשָּׁה חֻמְשֵׁי תוֹרָה. אַרְבַּע אִמָּהוֹת. שְׁלֹשָׁה אָבוֹת. שְׁנֵי לֻחוֹת הַבְּרִית אֶחָד אֱלֹהֵינוּ שֶׁבַּשָּׁמַיִם וּבָאָרֶץ:

חַד גַּדְיָא חַד גַּדְיָא דְּזַבֵּן אַבָּא בִּתְרֵי זוּזֵי. חַד גַּדְיָא חַד גַּדְיָא:

וְאָתָא שׁוּנְרָא וְאָכַל לְגַדְיָא דְּזַבֵּן אַבָּא בִּתְרֵי זוּזֵי. חַד גַּדְיָא חַד גַּדְיָא:

וְאָתָא כַלְבָּא. וְנָשַׁךְ לְשׁוּנְרָא. דְּאָכַל לְגַדְיָא. דְּזַבֵּן אַבָּא בִּתְרֵי זוּזֵי. חַד גַּדְיָא חַד גַּדְיָא:

וְאָתָא חוּטְרָא. וְהִכָּה לְכַלְבָּא. דְּנָשַׁךְ לְשׁוּנְרָא. דְּאָכַל לְגַדְיָא דְּזַבֵּן אַבָּא בִּתְרֵי זוּזֵי. חַד גַּדְיָא חַד גַּדְיָא:

וְאָתָא נוּרָא. וְשָׂרַף לְחוּטְרָא. דְּהִכָּה לְכַלְבָּא. דְּנָשַׁךְ לְשׁוּנְרָא. דְּאָכַל לְגַדְיָא. דְּזַבֵּן אַבָּא בִּתְרֵי זוּזֵי. חַד גַּדְיָא חַד גַּדְיָא:

וְאָתָא מַיָּא. וְכָבָה לְנוּרָא. דְּשָׂרַף לְחוּטְרָא. דְּהִכָּה לְכַלְבָּא. דְּנָשַׁךְ לְשׁוּנְרָא. דְּאָכַל לְגַדְיָא. דְּזַבֵּן אַבָּא בִּתְרֵי זוּזֵי. חַד גַּדְיָא חַד גַּדְיָא:

וְאָתָא תוֹרָא. וְשָׁתָא לְמַיָּא. דְּכָבָה לְנוּרָא. דְּשָׂרַף לְחוּטְרָא. דְּהִכָּה לְכַלְבָּא. דְּנָשַׁךְ לְשׁוּנְרָא. דְּאָכַל לְגַדְיָא דְּזַבֵּן אַבָּא בִּתְרֵי זוּזֵי. חַד גַּדְיָא חַד גַּדְיָא:

Had Gadya

One kid, one kid,
That father bought for two zuzim;
One kid, one kid.

Came a cat and ate the kid
That father bought for two zuzim;
One kid, one kid.

Came a dog and bit the cat
That ate the kid
That father bought for two zuzim;
One kid, one kid.

Came a stick and beat the dog
That bit the cat
That ate the kid
That father bought for two zuzim;
One kid, one kid.

Came a fire and burned the stick
That beat the dog
That bit the cat
That ate the kid
That father bought for two zuzim;
One kid, one kid.

Came the water and quenched the fire
That burned the stick
That beat the dog
That bit the cat
That ate the kid
That father bought for two zuzim;
One kid, one kid.

Came an ox and drank the water
That quenched the fire
That burned the stick
That beat the dog
That bit the cat
That ate the kid
That father bought for two zuzim;
One kid, one kid.

The Fifth Cup

The United Jewish Appeal, under the directorship of Rabbi Herbert A. Friedman, created a "Fifth Cup" ritual in 1972 to mark the start of the Soviet Jewry Exodus. As its meaning broadened during the 1970s, the ritual "underscored the responsibility of American Jews to the people of Israel everywhere."

Came the butcher and killed the ox
That drank the water
That quenched the fire
That burned the stick
That beat the dog
That bit the cat
That ate the kid
That father bought for two zuzim;
One kid, one kid.

Came the Angel of Death
And slew the butcher
Who killed the ox
That drank the water
That quenched the fire
That burned the stick
That beat the dog
That bit the cat
That ate the kid
That father bought for two zuzim;
One kid, one kid.

Came the Blessed Holy One
And slew the Angel of Death
Who slew the butcher
Who killed the ox
That drank the water
That quenched the fire
That burned the stick
That beat the dog
That bit the cat
That ate the kid
That father bought for two zuzim;
One kid, one kid.

וְאָתָא הַשּׁוֹחֵט. וְשָׁחַט לְתוֹרָא. דְּשָׁתָא לְמַיָּא. דְּכָבָה
לְנוּרָא. דְּשָׂרַף לְחוּטְרָא. דְּהִכָּה לְכַלְבָּא. דְּנָשַׁךְ
לְשׁוּנְרָא. דְּאָכַל לְגַדְיָא. דְּזַבֵּן אַבָּא בִּתְרֵי זוּזֵי. חַד
גַּדְיָא חַד גַּדְיָא:

וְאָתָא מַלְאַךְ הַמָּוֶת וְשָׁחַט לְשׁוֹחֵט דְּשָׁחַט לְתוֹרָא
דְּשָׁתָא לְמַיָּא דְּכָבָה לְנוּרָא דְּשָׂרַף לְחוּטְרָא דְּהִכָּה
לְכַלְבָּא דְּנָשַׁךְ לְשׁוּנְרָא דְּאָכַל לְגַדְיָא דְּזַבֵּן אַבָּא בִּתְרֵי
זוּזֵי חַד גַּדְיָא חַד גַּדְיָא:

וְאָתָא הַקָּדוֹשׁ בָּרוּךְ הוּא וְשָׁחַט לְמַלְאַךְ הַמָּוֶת דְּשָׁחַט
לְשׁוֹחֵט דְּשָׁחַט לְתוֹרָה דְּשָׁתָא לְמַיָּא דְּכָבָה לְנוּרָא
דְּשָׂרַף לְחוּטְרָא דְּהִכָּא לְכַלְבָּא דְּנָשַׁךְ לְשׁוּנְרָא דְּאָכַל
לְגַדְיָא דְּזַבֵּן אַבָּא בִּתְרֵי זוּזֵי. חַד גַּדְיָא חַד גַּדְיָא:

On a farm in Iowa, Bubbie weaves the tale of the Exodus for
her grandson. *Young Israel*, Cincinnati, Ohio, April, 1925

Passover Ads from The 19th Century

At the Passover Breakfast Table

Boston, April, 1926

H.P. HOOD & SONS MILK

HOOD

The 1920s and 1930s

PASSOVER GIFTS in U.S.S.R. (RUSSIA)

שלחו מתנות לחג הפסח

via RADIO or CABLE

לקרוביכם וידידיכם

ברוסיה הסוביטית

חנויות טורגסין מצויות בכל עיר גדולה בארץ הסוביטים

HaDoar Hebrew Weekly, New York, March 29, 1935

Win a Free Trip to Palestine!!
at one of 248 PRIZES
IN THE MANISCHEWITZ ESSAY CONTEST on "THE UPBUILDING OF PALESTINE"

A great contest!! A real opportunity for you. Get an Entry Blank from your grocer. Read the details.

לכבוד פסח MANISCHEWITZ MATZOS

MATZO MEAL · FARFEL · CAKE MEAL · EGG MATZO

The American Hebrew, New York, April 1934

Strictly Fresh Fish

The "Seder" ceremony will be enjoyed by you and your family when you serve *Sol Cantor's Fresh Fish*. Remember the place, Center corner Fullerton Street. 82 car or 85 car brings you in front of our store.

Grant 9051   Telephone   Main 726

The Jewish Criterion,
Pittsburgh, Pennsylvania, April, 1921

Handbill from Atlanta, Georgia, March 1935.

Coca-Cola Now Kosher For Passover

Coca-Cola

קאקא קאלא כשר פיר פסח

Rabbi TOBIAS GEFFEN

The Passover Pause That Refreshes

A Bottle cap with certification by Rabbi Tobias Geffen 1935

הגדה
של פסח

★

AGADAH

PASSOVER SEDER SERVICE

★

Compliments of

COCA-COLA BOTTLING CO.

THE PAUSE THAT REFRESHES

KOSHER FOR PASSOVER

Memphis, Tennessee, Coca-Cola bottling Co. 1936

ושמחת בחגך

אכול כל סעודות הפסח
בשמחה ושתה בכל
סעודה וסעודה
„קוקה ‘קולה”
דוקא בבקבוקים אשר
ימצא על הפקק
„כשר J.B. לפסח תרצ”א”
כי רק *Coca-Cola* באלה
הבקבוקים כשר לפסח
בעיר ניו-יורק וסביבותיה
יעקב
„קוקה ‘קולה”
הוא באוצר בנוסח
בפסח.
כל ירא-שמים יכול להביא
את גופו במשקה
ה„קוקה קולה”
הכשר הנ”ל.
קנה די ספוקך לכל
ימי החג במחיר
הנהוג בכל השנה.

COCA COLA BOTTLING CO., N. Y.

"Rejoice in your festival with Coca Cola, the same price on the holiday as the rest of the year" *HaDoar* Hebrew Weekly, New York, April 1931

Matzo Kleis

Soak four matzos in cold water, and press them after being thoroughly saturated. Add a little pepper, salt, sugar, parsley, and half an onion chopped fine, first browning the onion. Beat four eggs, and add all together. Then put in enough matzo meal so that it may be rolled into balls. The less meal used the lighter will be the balls. They should boil about twenty minutes before serving.   (1901)

Sole with Wine
(French recipe).

Take a sole or fillets of any delicate fish. Lay on a fireproof dish, sprinkling with white pepper, salt and a little shalot, cover with claret or white wine, and let it cook in the oven till done. Draw off the liquor in a saucepan, and let it boil up. Have ready the yolks of three eggs, well stirred (not beaten). the juice of a lemon, and two ounces of butter. Put all together in a bowl. Little by little add the hot sauce, stirring all the time. Pour it over the fish, and sprinkle with chopped parsley. Serve very hot. A few mushrooms are a palatable addition to this dish.   (1898)

Kentucky Gremslich

Two and half cups of meal, four eggs, two cups of sugar, one kitchen-spoon of goose fat, one of beef fat, four apples, and spices

Recipes

from The American Hebrew, March 1898 and April 1901

The American way – clip the coupons for instant savings on Passover products such as coffee, pitted prunes, muffin mix and lox

according to taste. One wine glass of wine also, if convenient. Put the meal in a bowl with salt, pepper, ground clove, allspice and cinnamon mixed into it; peel and grate the apples, melt the fat and mix, put in the eggs and then stir in the sugar which had been boiled with water to a thin syrup and cooled off. Hollow out two pieces, put cranberries or any fruit between them; form into

balls the size of a medium apple, and bake them on a well-greased pie-plate for about one hour.
(1901)

Palestine Soup

Three pounds of Jerusalem artichokes, two quarts of real stock, one turnip, one head of celery, pepper and salt to taste. Peel and cut the vegetables into slices and boil them in the stock till tender, then rub through a hair sieve. Beat the yolks of three eggs, add to the soup. and stir over the fire till just on the boil. The soup should be about the thickness of rich cream. If not thick enough, a little potato flour may be added.
(1901)

Matzo Shalet

Three soaked matzos, 9 eggs, 1 cup of sugar, 2 grated apples 1 1/2 cups seeded raisins, 1 tablespoon cinnamon, grated rind of an orange or a lemon and a few pounded almonds. Beat the sugar, eggs and cinnamon until light, then add all the ingredients, except the matzos, mixing well. Now drain the matzos, gradually adding them to the mixture, beating until very light, Melt half a pound of rendered fat into the dish for baking, and then pour in the mixture, bake in a moderately hot oven for 1 1/4 hours. Serve hot — with wine, fruit or prune sauce.   (1901)

The Passover Tradition Continues

SEE SPECIALLY MARKED PACKAGES WITH (K) P

KOSHER
FOR
PASSOVER
IN SPECIALLY
MARKED
PACKAGES
WITH (K) P
LIMITED QUANTITIES

New York's
THIRD SEDER

On April 5, 1942, the New York friends of the Histadrut Labor Federation held a Third Seder to pledge "their loyalty to the modern redemption" of Eretz Yisrael. 5,000 people attended the Seder at its two locations: The Astor and Commodore Hotels. The speakers shown here, left to right: Rabbi Stephen Wise, David Pinski, Louis Segal, David Ben Gurion and Senator Elbert D. Thomas. For the evening $125,000 was raised.

The Peculiar Observances of Today

"At 12:30 o'clock last night," explained a communicative Hebrew, "the Jews left Egypt without leaven for their bread, and it is in commemoration of the flight that we hold this feast. We eat nothing that has leaven or yeast in it for eight days. They are all impure. But we eat everything else. The fact is, we live better during the eight days than other time of the year. We drink no beer, but we use wine and all kinds of meats, the prescription being restricted to dishes or beverages in which leaven has been used."

Every Evening, Wilmington, Delaware, March 26, 1888

Seder in Kansas City

"The night of the first seder found the big table in the dining room in our home in Kansas City, Missouri set with our special Pesach set of dishes and the "bechers" (kiddush cups) for Papa and our five brothers as well as for extra guests who were always invited. Papa's seder plate was at the head of the table with all the required items including the ingredients for Charoseth waiting for Papa to mix it (the chopped apples, cinnamon, sweet red wine and ground walnuts — the nuts Papa 'ground' by hitting them with a small hammer as they were bound in a fresh white cloth).

"The kitchen exuded glorious aromas, and, of course, there was a fluffy eight-egg Pesach sponge cake for dessert and perhaps some 'imberlach' — a ginger candy Mama made. Kosher dairy products were brought to Kansas City from the Raskas Dairy Company in St. Louis, Missouri."

Mrs. Shoshana Dolgin Be'er, Jerusalem

Passover in Atlanta during the Depression

"Despite the Depression, Passover was a vibrant time in the Atlanta Jewish community in the 1930s. For a month before the holiday the smell of cleaning permeated the house, to be supplanted by the delicious cooking odors as the holiday neared.

"At the seder, the first part of the Haggadah was read in detail and with feeling, but after the holiday meal with its unusual dishes, the younger generation tried to hurry up the reading and the verbal explanations. In fact, it was only the expectation of the hunt for the Afikoman and the subsequent reward that kept the youngest group at the table. At the end, it was the singing of the Haggadah melodies that were the most fun, and some of those tunes remain with me to this day.

"We stayed out of school for the first two and last two days of Passover, of course. During Chol Hamoed we went to school, bringing matzah sandwiches and fruit for lunch. No Jew would eat bread during that period, and certainly not in public. Commercial High School, which I attended, had enough Jews so that matzah was not uncommon, while non-Jewish students would sometimes ask for a taste of that peculiar Jewish cardboard."

David Macarov, Ph.D.
Professor Emeritus, Hebrew University, Jerusalem

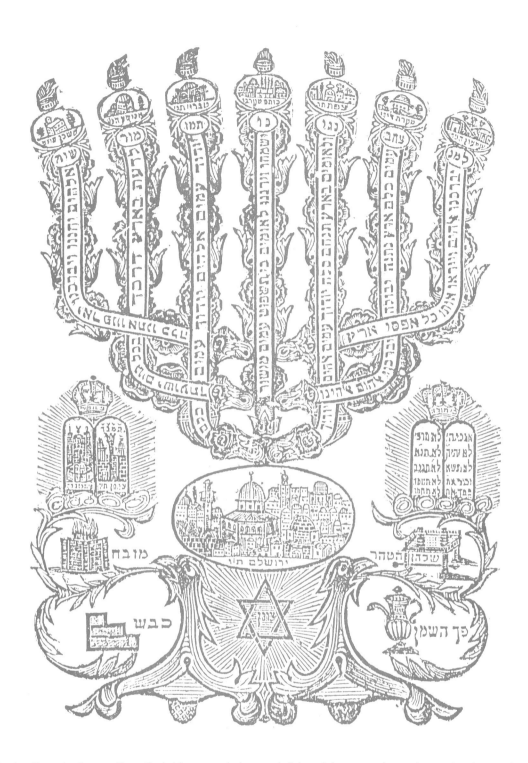

This illustration is from the first Haggadah published by an American in Jerusalem. The publisher, Yitzhak Nahum Levi, concluded the book with these sentiments:

"May he be remembered for glory, Rabbi Benjamin Gittelsohn of Cleveland. From a distance, the United States, he provided work for the inhabitants of Jerusalem, so that they might enjoy the labor of their hands. And praise to the Lord, we have completed the printing with beauty, clear letters, and good paper. And this should be a sign to our brethren that the work of our printing plant is very outstanding. And we hope that all Jews will learn from him and whoever has something to print, will send it to us, and with God's help we will fulfill every request. In addition, they will strengthen the Jewish community in Palestine in a noble and elegant manner."

Haggadah for Passover
Jerusalem, 1904.

פסח

SEDER
1945·5705
PGC

Ft. Sill, Oklahoma

Passover 1955

HARDBOILED EGGS
(o)

EYER MIT ZVIBEL MIT GEHOCKTE LEBUR
(a la' hachshoosh)

KNEDIECH SOUP
(a la' Iran)

TOHA TOES
OLIVES

CHREHSLECH
(no kidding)

GOLDEN APPLES

IANNA FROM HEAVEN
(a la' Baghdad)
MUNNISANA

CH' LASS
L'SHANA HA'BAWAH B'U.S.A.

(Arabic)
SALTWA TER
soy)

ASPARAGUS
PEAS

ICED TEA

Wiliam Kaplae .... APO 689
Markus Genra .... APO 706   Leaders
Marshall Cohen .... APO 706

RALPH M. WEISBERGER .... Chaplain

1944 PERSIAN GULF COMMAND
הקומנדו האמריקאי במרץ הפרסי תש"ד

263

די סדר נאכט

SEDER NACHT

CHILDREN'S SONG

PATRIOTIC SONG

Madame Sophia Karp

COMPOSED BY
LOUIS FRIEDSELL

NEW YORK
THEODORE LOHR
266 GRAND ST

HAGGADAH
for the
LIBERATED LAMB

PASSOVER
פסח

בדיקת חמץ

הגדה

Passover Greetings ~ חג שמח

PLEASE
KEEP OFF

DO NOT STUB OUT
CIGARETTE ENDS ON
PLASTIC DECKING

MENU

~Lettuce~

Potatoes~Saltwater

~Eggs~

~Gefilte Fish~

~Chopped Liver~

Chicken Soup~Matzoh Farfel

~Roast Chicken~

Peas ~ Carrots

~Khremslech~

Nuts ~ Olives ~ Fruit

~Iced Tea~

East Side
Branch
151
EAST BROADWAY

Main Office
85-99 HUDSON ST
A LYBARSKI
Manager

וכבה תאכלו אותו

Enjoying a cup of Wissotzky's
Russian tea after the SEDER

Please mention THE AMERICAN HEBREW when writing to or dealing with our Advertisers.